Foreword

And then I decided to put it all in one volume,
I could keep writing until they air season six.
And then call it a day...........but It seems complete to the end of
season five and a little bit further.

This volume is all of my Outlander related work, put In some sort of
chronological order to tell a story,
Some readers will have read some of my efforts before, but much of it
is new, at least to publication.
It is not an official Outlander product.

Credit is due to Diana Gabaldon - the stories and characters are hers,
I hope I have told them from a different perspective and with a poetic
spin.

Again I thank the Facebook Outlander Fan Pages on which I appear.
They have provided, endless support, boosted morale, critiqued,
provided guidance on content, and corrected punctuation and
spelling.

Thank you.

Table of Contents   Page

Obsession   6
Outlanders Progress   8
The Next Thrilling Instalment   10
Where we learn to swim   13
Oh Carolina   16
Two sorts of Theatre in one   19
Here's some more season four   22
We survive to season five   25
A snake, maggots and a buffalo   29
The land before the drought   32
Watching the Rugby (Wales v Scotland)   37
Domestic Update   39
Modern Day Jamie   41
The Lads Night Out   43

Introduction to Part 2 - a journey through the stones   44

Palmistry   45
Jamies Ghost   46
Claire   47
Confusion   49
A Long Ride   51
Redcoats   53
The Devils Right Hand Man   54
The First Visit   56
Flogging   58
Alex Macgregors Bible.   60
My Godfather   61
Machiavelliam   63
Angus Mhor   65
Mor Angus !   67

Rupert Thomas Alexander Mackenzie	68
A Man of Letters	69
The Laird and His Wife	71
A Woman Scorned	73
The Full Scottish	75
Planning a Wedding	77
Second Time Around	79
The Wedding Night	81
Gaberlunzie	83
Locked in Time	85
Self Defence	86
A Rare Old Sodomite	88
Drama In the Hall	90
Cranesmuir	92
The Witch	94
Jenny Murray	96
Ian Murray	98
The Laird has a Hangover	100
Fixing the Mill	101
A Visit from the Watch	103
On the Run	105
The Aftermath	107
A Hot Bath	109
A Rough Crossing	110
The Bonnie Prince	111
Parisian to the Core	112
Eat a Healthy Breakfast	114
Master Raymond	115
Idle Hands	117
Loss of Faith	119
The Old Fox	121
Carryarick	123
Preston Pans	125

Culloden	127
Half a life	130
Ian the Wanderer	132
The Dun Bonnet	134
Ardsmuir to Helwater	136
Life at Ardsmuir	139
Helwater and Back	141
Geneva has a Plan	144
The 9th Earl - Willie	146
Finding Jamie	148
Thoughts in Print	151
Kidnapped	154
Acupuncture	156
The Porpoise	157
Father Fogden	159
Lord John Gets it Right	161
Ians Rescue	164
Drowning	165
Shipwrecked	166
The things you win at Dice	167
Burying Hayes	169
Robbed	171
Aunt Jocasta	174
Bear Killer	176
Finding the Ridge.	177
Lizzie	179
On Finding my Father	181
A Fish Out of Water	184
The Privy	186
Being Willie	188
The White Sow	191
Regulators	193
Goats and Hell	195

Bitten by a Snake	198
Rape	201
I've Taken No Such Oath	203
The Coming Storm	205
Taking Stock	206
Bedtime Stories	207
The End of my World	209
Forget me Not	211

Obsession.

I don't watch that much TV.
I'd rather read a book,
But lockdowns given me spare time
So I thought I'd take a look.

I'm into things historical
I like a bit of drama.
What's this series Outlander ?
That Jamie looks a charmer.

So, I ventured through the stones
To Jacobites and scandal.
I winced at Wentworth prison
And I hated Black Jack Randall.

I laughed at angry Angus
Rupert made me chuckle.
And listened hard to Murtagh
What on earth is Muckle (it's big)

I've gotten mad with Dougal.
He's a fanatic and a schemer.
I've fallen out with Laoghaire.
The fantasist and dreamer.

And as for Jamie Fraser
I've thought things I must not mention
My husband calls him kilt porn.
And laughs at my obsession

I've started drinking whiskey
And talking with a lilt
I've started calling small things wee
What's worn under the kilt ?

I don't watch it for the sex scenes,
That's just an ugly rumour.
I love the twinkle in old Murtaghs eye
And Jamie's sense of humour.

Tortured, beaten, broken
Claire puts him back together
Safe hands to hold his mortal soul
Bound to him forever.

***

The Outlanders progress

I'm into series two now
The Frasers are in Paris
My whisky habits getting worse
A wee dram is a habit.

My house is turning tartan
I've throws on every chair
My screen saver is Jamie
And most of him is bare!

I hum the theme, the Skye Boat song
When I do the cleaning.
I iron with the series on
In case I've missed a hidden meaning.

What is the score with Jamie's ghost?
Why is he watching Claire?
When will Bees be finished?
When will the new stuff air?

I've looked up local courses
To learn the Gaelic tongue.
I had a problem learning Welsh
My languages aren't strong – ye Ken

It makes me laugh
It makes me run the gamut of emotions,
It's effects are so much stronger
Than one of Claire's best potions.

So I will binge on Outlander
Shamelessly watch it back
Pour another dram my friend
And call me Sassenach.

Slainte

****

The Next Thrilling Instalment

As I progress to Season three
We've lost a few old friends.
Angus died at Preston Pans
Dougal murdered at the end.

Culloden is upon us
Will Jamie make Claire go,
To live in safety, back with Frank
I think we sort of know!

I've acquired a set of glasses,
In a Jacobean style
A present from my husband
They really make me smile.

I've bought myself a broadsword,
With a basket hilt
I may use it on my husband
If he won't wear the kilt !

And Jamie's back in Lallybroch
Living in a cave.
And Fergus gets his hand chopped off
By Red Coats on the rave.

Young Ian's birth sees Red Coats
Arriving in a hurry
Ian lies in Jamie's arms
More Fraser than a Murray.

My lovely husbands sulking
He's gone off in a huff.
The life size Jamie Fraser
in the bedroom was enough!

I tried to tell him Dinna Fash
He said I'd lost the plot
But he's dug out his old weights bench
And he's training quite a lot !

There's all sorts of revelations,
Claire finds out that he survived
She travels through the stones again
To find him still alive.

The bastard married Laoghaire
Don't tell me Dinna Fash!
She's turned up in Lallybroch
And started a stramash!

She took a gun to Jamie
She shot him in the arm.
But Claire is there to heal him
He won't come to any harm.

Ned comes to the rescue,
To sort the legal stuff
Laoghaire just wants money
And his bollocks – ooh that's rough.

Maybe I'll buy parchment
And start writing with a quill
Lots goes on in season three
So I don't think I will.

As I sink my late night dram
And make my way to bed,
I come across my husband,
Highland bonnet on his head.

Is that a kilt he's wearing?
Are there scars upon his back ?
I'll know I'm on a promise,
If he calls me Sassenach!

****

Where we learn to Swim

Season three – the second half
Involves a lot of water
A search for buried treasure
Tartan swimsuit is on order.

Young Ian swims to get the jewels
The Bakra captures Ian.
Jamie sails to save him
We are off to the Caribbean.

Claire is press-ganged (for want of a better expression) - by the Navy
Cures the crew of blazing shits
Typhoid is a killer
Rips your arse to bits

Jamie is in danger
They found the body in the cask.
He's wanted for a murder
Claire must escape to warn him
Fast!

Not to mention Father Fogden!
Now that would be a crime.
Where did I put that coconut
It's conversation time.

Fergus marries Marsali
It's romantic – on the sand.
Fergus becomes a Fraser
With a cock and no left hand!

My hubby is in the kitchen
My house smells like the sea
With an awful lot of Sherry
Oh my ......there's turtle soup for tea.

(Bolt the door! ....)

The father of my daughter
Is a very lovely man...
May be a closet Outlander
But he's right there on the plan.

We've landed in Jamaica
The Naval Captain is a Cock.
He sends a troop of soldiers
To arrest Jamie - on the Dock

But a temporary Captain
Is no match for him I fear.
We are up before the Governor
Oh look Lord John is here.

Ian is in danger -
the Bakra (that's a white slave owner) has him In a cave
Her fetish is for virgin boys
Young Ian is her slave

And here's another friend returned
The Bakra looks like someone
Bathed in blood and witchcraft
Oh my it's Geilis Duncan.

And off they sail into a storm
Where our hero's should have died
But at least they find America
On the other side.

****

Oh Carolina

So here I am still writing,
And here comes season four.
We've reached the Carolinas
The Frasers are on Tour !

Meanwhile in obsession land
I've started eating Parritch
I don't really want the problem
King Louis had in Paris.

The spare room has been fitted out
With stone walls and bars and chains
My husband is responsible
He always takes such pains.

I'm not sure of his motives
Oh Lord John! What can I say?
I think he's got it mixed up
With 50 shades of Grey.

Less of my domestic strife
Let's get back to the plot.
Things don't go well for our friend Hayes
But Bonnet slips the knot!

Never fall for Irish charm
Or as they call it Blarney
Bonnet is a wicked man
Jamie you were Barmy

Robbed of all except their clothes
Claire's rings are swallowed twice,
Young Ian has acquired a dog
Rollo – he won him playing dice.

River Run is quite a pad.
Jocasta a MacKenzie,
She needs a man to run the show
She could leave the lot to Jamie.

But Claire is anti slavery,
This is a deal breaker
Jamie isn't all that keen,
He doesn't try to make her.

A deal is done with Tryon
For an acreage of land
I think it's big as the whole of Wales
That's where they make their stand.

Meanwhile back in our time
Brianna makes a find
Her parents death, an epitaph
They both die in a fire.

She leaves a note for Roger,
And heads off for the stones.
Hoping to warn her parents
That they may not make 'old bones'

Meanwhile up on Frasers ridge
The Indians call around,
Seems Scots and Native Indians
Can share a common ground.

A cabin built for shelter
Some livestock and a bed
A fight with a half crazed Indian bear
That's how Fraser life is led.

Meanwhile Roger finds the note
And goes in search of Bree
And meets with Captain Bonnet
And journeys across the sea.

They all end up in Wilmington
Including dopey Lizzie
Hold on to your kilts my friends
The next part will be busy

****

Two sorts of Theatre in one

Wilmington is buzzing,
It's the hub of polite society,
But it still has a dark side
And loads of impropriety.

The Frasers are about in town
Going to the Theatre.
Tucking in a hernia
Thrills the public better.

And while all this is going on
Roger gets to town.
Surprises Young Brianna
Makes dopey Lizzie frown.

Bree and Roger quarrel
Bree sends him away,
But he's tied to Bonnets crew
Bonnet won't let him stay.

Then Bree gets raped by Bonnet
Tries buying back Claire's ring
Lizzie thinks that it was Roger
Though she didn't see a thing.

But the morning after
Lizzie nails it down.
It's she who finds the Frasers
Haven't yet left the town.

If you had to meet the father
You hadn't met at all,
Would you really like to meet him
Pissing up against a wall !

The Family is United
They start the journey home,
But what of poor old Roger
Still working his fingers to the bone.

Quick domestic update
I'm out of Sassenach!
There's some cheap stuff in the cupboard
Hiding at the back.

I've researched my family history
Are there Scots? The answers yes!
Someone married a McGregor
They came from Inverness.

My ever loving husband
Has begun to decorate
He's stuck my Jamie to the ceiling.
And I've ordered Tartan paint!

Back at the ridge
Claire has sussed Brianna is not 'right,'
She not just missing Roger
She cannot sleep at night.

But ever resourceful Roger,
Has made his own way back.
Lizzie sees him coming
Half way up the track.

You stupid thing, if your not sure
You really didn't aught to.
Tell a man like Jamie Fraser.
That's the man that raped your daughter!

There was no interrogation
No chance to explain.
A battle hardened iron fist
Can inflict so much pain

Ian took him off the ridge
And before he had time to talk
Roger had been sold a slave
To a branch of the Mohawk.

That's enough excitement
It's time to take a break
Then we'll go and look for Roger
And put right the mistake.

****

And here's some more of season four.

It's all been very hectic,
I'm still in season four.
Rogers with the Mohawk
That won't end well, I'm sure.

The Frasers pack the wagon
Take Bree to River Run.
Rogers walking far to New York
He's not having so much fun.

Jamie, Claire and Ian
Mount up and off they go
To try and buy our Roger back
I hope it doesn't snow.

Meanwhile I've acquired
A doorstop highland Coo,
A tin of Highland Shortbread,
And a Targue that's nearly new.

My sword is still hung on the wall
My Dirk is by the fire
Along with a large sheepskin rug
An object of desire.

My husbands brandishing his belt
I don't think he wants to thank me
I've strengthened up my throwing arm
In case he tries to spank me.

Brianna reads the letter
Jamie left with Lord John Grey,
He talks about forgiveness
She takes it the wrong way.

Bonnet has been captured
He's languishing in prison,
Bree gets Lord John to take her there
And Bonnet is forgiven.

But some of the regulators
Are locked up in the jail
They need to get their people out
And with a plan that cannot fail.....

They blow the bloody doors off
The jail in just a minute!
Leaving but a pile of wood
And Bonnet .... Isn't in it

Meanwhile up in New York State
Things have gone astray
They've rescued Roger from the tribe
But Young Ian chose to stay.

Rogers in a quandary
Claire's told him about Bree
Will he make a commitment
Or run off home ..... we'll see.

And so they're back at River Run
And the baby has arrived
Brees' got engaged to good Lord John
To avoid what Jocasta has contrived.

When the Frasers get there
Travelling without Ian.
Bree's waiting there for Roger
But he's not come ......read on

The Frasers have packed the Wagon
And they're leaving for the ridge
Oh look – here comes Roger
Riding cross the bridge.

✳✳✳✳

We survive to season five

So we all survived to season five,
We lived through season four,
I'll deal with my domestic stuff
Before I do much more.

Suffice to say my husband
Is downstairs with the duster.
Listening to my singing
Was more than he could muster.

He's been busy in the garden
Piling leaves up with a rake.
There's a huge pole and some kindling
And Oh my god a stake.

I think he's called the inquirers.
I think there's been a snitch.
I made him eat his mushrooms
Will he burn me as a witch!

On Frasers Ridge in season five
Lord Tryon is flexing muscle
He's after regulators
We can expect a tussle.

Brianna marries Roger
In a Presbyterian wedding
Jamie thinks they're hairy ticks
Cos the service ain't in Latin

Lord Tryon brings his soldiers
To camp on Fraser land
He's really after Murtagh
He intends to make a stand

Jamie calls the Clan out
To inspire loyalty
Oh my word the man is dressed
Like sexy highland royalty.

Jocasta takes another husband
To run her large estate.
She leaves it all to Jemmie
That rather seals his fate.

Bonnet bribes the lawyer
For details of the will.
He wants his paws on River Run
The lawyer is a schill.

Raising a militia is
where we meet the Browns
They all live in Brownsville
A most incestuous town.

We find the Beardsley cabin
Complete with a dying man.
A pregnant abused woman,
And a goat, completes the plan

The Beardsley mess is sorted.
They find the Twins their papers.
Mrs Beardsley does a runner,
It's enough to give the vapours

Recruiting for militia,
Don't you think that, maybe
Jamie had a big surprise
To come back with a baby.

In pursuit of regulators
Tryon stands at Alamance
Jamie tries to warn old Murtagh
He doesn't stand a chance.

Roger goes behind the lines
To tell him what History knows,
But Roger is no soldier and
With Buck Mackenzie comes to blows.

Oh that bastard Tryon
It really should be said
That was a nasty low down stroke you pulled
With that Coat of English Red.

Alamance is decisive
The regulators beat.
One of his men shoots Murtagh
Jamie's grief complete.

And where the hell is Roger
Where the bloody hell is he
Whilst making an example
Red Coats have hanged him from a tree.

Not the end for Roger
When they cut him down
Claire finds he is still breathing.
But his airway is closed down.

She opens up his windpipe
So his breath won't cause him pain
In doing so she makes it
So he never sings again.

There's a lot of mental healing
In the wake of Alamance
Ian returns to the Ridge.
He and Roger – mental health bromance

Time for a break in season five
My husbands cooking tea
When he's finished watching rugby
Scotland v England on TV

✳✳✳✳

A snake, maggots and a buffalo.

Going hunting for the ridge
To keep the larder stocked.
Jamie calls for Brianna sure shot
But gets Roger – who is half cocked.

Roger is not a marksman,
He can hardly aim a gun,
Or hit a cows arse with a shovel
Shooting buffalo should be fun.

Stalking through the forest
They come across the herd.
Then Jamie steps upon a snake.
Was that a curse I heard?

Jamie's slowly dying
He's really in a hole.
His leg is slowly festering
And snake venom takes its toll.

Roger will not let him die
He really plays his part.
He pulls him on a stretcher
Which is a work of art.

He's sucked the poison from his leg,
Applied a tourniquet.
If he can get home fast enough
James may fight another day.

The leg is in a bad old way
It gets a bit chaotic,
Claire has no syringe left
To inject antibiotic.

Our man ain't very happy
His leg is very sore.
Claire may have to take his leg off
Jamie hides the saw.

The ridge are hunting maggots
To eat the dying flesh.
Brianna to the rescue
With a proper brilliant flash.

Roger kept the snakes head
He kept it in his bag.
Snakes inject their poison
Through a sharp and hollow fang.

This Heath Robinson invention
May just save the day,
Claire is keeping her man warm
In a most unusual way.

Enter wounded Buffalo
It gives Lizzie a fright.
Well done Claire for shooting it
There's steak for tea tonight.

Let's return to our hero's leg
Claire has got her kit.
She jabs the fang into his wound
It made him wince a bit.

A bit of penicillin
Does wonders against germs
And a snakes fang jabbed into yer arse
Will really make you squirm.

Our hero's leg now on the mend
Claire says he must stay still,
Maybe he's reading poetry
That I've written with my quill.

✳✳✳

The land before the Drought

Scotland has beaten England (in the rugby at Twickenham)
And I have had my tea
Hubby bought a tidy bottle
So I have a dram by me .... slainte

There's a pause at Frasers Ridge
We turn the plot to Bonnet,
His plan to steal River Run
And all that rests upon it.

Bonnet thinks he's Jemmies dad
Bree and Roger Mac weren't wed.
Bree had turned the Lawyer down
And engaged Lord John instead.

In a bid for Jemmies custody
Bonnet must clean up his act.
Curtail his worse behaviour
Play the gent in fact.

They plan a nasty accident
For Jocasta any day
So Bonnet can get River Run
And the lawyer gets his pay.

Roger Ian and Jamie
Intend to shove a hand in
On the pretext of a Whiskey deal
With Bonnet at Wylies landing.

But Bonnet doesn't show up
He's lying really low
In a house nearby an island
Where you can see the Whales blow.

He knocks Claire unconscious
And leaves her on the beach.
Then kidnaps Bree and takes her
Somewhere he thinks she's out of reach.

There is a rescue mission
When did Roger learn to punch?
Bonnet is arrested
And the Crocs can have their lunch.

Ulysess saves Jocasta
And then goes on the run.
The lawyer is killed while visiting
Out at River Run.

All is not quite quiet
As the Browns are on the way.
Young Ian knows of time travel
And Lord John comes to stay.

Peanut Butter is on the menu
And now it's time to talk
About a peanut butter sandwich
And a knife and fork!.

The Ridge has said a fond goodbye
To Bree and Roger Mac.
They're going off to "Boston"
And they're not coming back

Lionel Brown is an evil man,
He's broken his wife's arm.
Dr Rawlings sound advice
Is the cause of the alarm.

Was it strange the still blew up
The day the Brown gang came.
They kidnapped Claire and
Trashed the place –
what could be their game.

Tied up, beaten, tortured, raped
Claire's outlook is all black.
Thank god that she has Jamie
To glue the pieces back.

The fiery cross is set alight
Jamie calls the clan.
The ridge turn out to back him
Loyal to a man.

Our man has got his kilt on
This no fashionable decision.
There will be no prisoners
On this rescue mission.

And Roger Mac and Bree are back.
When they thought of home.
Despite the fact they disappeared
They went nowhere through the stone.

Kill them all! - they've found the Browns
Ruthless to the core.
There's one survivor – Lionel
Taken for questioning and more.

Tied down to the table
In the surgery at the house,
Lionel is helpless
And as quiet as a mouse.

Claire may do no harm to him
By Hypocratic oath.
But Marsali is not bound by this
She can avenge them both.

She quietly steeps the hemlock
And when he starts to wheedle.
She loads it up in the syringe
And injects it through the needle.

Thunder rolls across the hills
The coming of a storm.
The Frasers will repair themselves
Safe in each other's arms.

There is no more to write about
The Bees are not yet humming.
Load and prime your muskets
There's a revolution coming.

Hubby has gone up the stairs
I'm typing on my own
Guess I shall pour a dram
Put Outlander on
And watch it all alone.........
🚩 🏳️iechyd da.........🚩   slainte mhath.

Watching the Rugby (Wales v Scotland)

Yesterday was Saturday
In Wales we watched the game.
Scotland up in Murrayfield
A match that's never tame.

A nail biting first half
Scotland 9 points ahead
Wales will have their work cut out
Come on the men in red.

Watching on the pod cast
I recognise that man
It's John Quincy Myers
Ah ..... so that's how they got Sam.

Half time we get Sam on
Gloating quite a bit.
He's wearing Heughan no 10
He likes his Scottish Kit.

My husband has me rumbled.
Pod cast ! he says ,that's new
You've only got that thing on
Because he's in Outlander too.

Shut up and watch the rugby
It's getting quite exciting
They must have had a row at half time.
Wales have come out fighting.

My daughter tells me to calm down
I'm shouting at the screen
Mum the ref can't hear you!
And your language is obscene!

Wales won! We can't believe it.
But only by one point.
I'd love to see Sam Heughans face
Do Scottish disappointed

Come to Wales next year,
Will we see you in the crowd.
Best you bring your ear plugs
The Welsh can cheer quite loud.

****

Domestic Update

Here's a little update
On the course of my affliction.
I wake up thinking Gaelic
And talk in Scottish diction!

I tried to swap the duvet
For some sheepskins and a quilt.
And keep a blade under the mattress
Where I can reach the hilt.

My hubby looks like Dougal
He's bald and wears a beard.
But his humour is like Rupert,
This makes life pretty weird.

I know he's planning something
I can read his heid.
He's scouring the free ads.
For a coat of red.

He's learned to fire a musket,
The lessons were quite odd
He doesn't quite know what to do,
With that great ramrod.

He talks a lot, of powder,
And a lot, of balls (he talks a lot of it anyway)
There's a five foot Brown Bess musket,
Propped up in my hall.

We've had a lot of rain in Wales,
The garden is quite sodden.
Has he asked some friends round.
To re-enact Culloden?

****

Modern Day Jamie

If Jamie could walk through the stones
Into modern times,
What would he be, how would he cope?
I thought I'd write a rhyme,

He was born a farmers son,
Taught to work the land,
But he's equally as happy
With a broadsword in his hand.

He's handsome and intelligent,
And very down to earth,
And he's very good with horses,
He's worked with them since birth.

He has a problem with authority,
A temper which can kill,
He'll fight you all one handed,
He also has that skill.

He's at his best on solid ground,
He doesn't like the sea.
He's not an ideal candidate for
Joining the navy.

He's the handsome red haired bad boy,
Standing by the bar,
The one who buys you all a drink,
And drives an awesome car.

The girls go weak before him,
But he's loyal to his chick,
Don't try and steal his property,
He'll deck you, double quick.

He would not cope with modern day,
There's far to many rules,
Old fashioned, and rebellious,
He falls between two stools.

He'd have to learn about the law.
Then when your hopes have risen.
Just as you thought you'd got him tamed
He'd end up in prison.

✳✳✳✳

The lads night out

It was my ghostly birthday,
Beltane here again
Gone down the town for a few drams,
Wi the lads ye ken.

The boys had left me on my own,
Off in search of lassies,
I thought I'd get a wee kebab
And then go for a taxi.

I hauled up by the monument,
I needed a wee rest,
And saw her in a window,
Combing out a nest.

My heid was a confusion,
I didna feel sae clever,
But that lass in the window,
Was mine, I knew for ever.

Who is this boring looking man,
He's seen me I'm a fearing,
I'm just admiring a good view
Why is he interfering.

Ach there are nae taxis
I must get home of course,
It's a long old way to Leoch,
Best I steal a horse !

****

Part 2

Take a wander through the stones with me,
All from my perspective,
My take on the characters,
Most of it objective.

Written during lockdown,
To keep myself amused,
I hope none of the characters
Feel they've been abused.

You've caught up on the plot so far,
They're filming season six.
Part one contained some humour,
We like to have a mix.

There is lots of new stuff
To help you muddle through,
Until that book called bees comes out.
Welcome to Part Two.

Palmistry

Handed down the generations
A gift, or maybe skill ?
Prophecy, or witchcraft,
Call it what you will.

Everyone is born with lines
Engraved upon their hand.
Does each hidden meaning.
Show your destiny is planned?

The lines which one is born with
Are just a basic outline,
Life will add some twists and turns
As you journey down your timeline.

Some marker posts may be laid out,
You may not choose that highway,
Some detours may be added.
Some lay-bys and some byways.

Your palm is on a journey
It fits you like a glove.
Is it's basic layout planned.
By some power up above?

Is it fate, or is it luck?
A Freeman or a slave,
Is our lifetime all mapped out?
From the cradle to the grave.

****

Jamie's Ghost

I saw her in a mirror
A reflection from afar,
A face as clear as Crystal
Eyes as bright as stars.

Hair around her shoulders
Thick to choke the comb
Bonnie Brown and gleaming
Ah Mo Nighean Donn.

I watch her from the roadside
My heart and soul are gone.
This night when I can wander
When chains of time are none.

Must I wait two hundred years
'Til she can lie with me
Until our time is one again
And her spirit is set free?

I must go – I have been seen
I'm tied in time forever
Forget me not – my Bonnie Lass
Our bond will never sever

****

Claire

Brought up by my Uncle Lamb,
Most unusual for the day.
We travelled and I learned of life
I learned to make my own way.

A streak of independence,
That wouldn't yet conform.
A drive to do things with my life
Not live it in the norm.

A marriage during wartime
Is hard to keep together.
Not seeing him for many years
Made it heavy weather.

And I saw more of War than him,
He was behind the scenes.
I saw the bodies and the blood
It's me who has those dreams.

Frank was my first love,
But not one to the end.
After the war, when he came back
He was more like a friend.

For the sake of continuity
We tacked us back together
Tried to start where we left off.
It would never last forever.

I didn't mean to fall for him
Fall through the veil of time,
A thing bigger than both of us
Meant him to be mine.

We know each other's inner thoughts,
Read each other's mind.
Know when each is feeling pain
Know which wounds to bind.

Death can never cut the cord
The bond death cannot sever
Blood of blood, bone of bone,
I'm bound to you forever.

****

Confusion

So my wife is pregnant,
I am overjoyed!
Nice to see while she was away
She was gainfully employed.

If I am to believe her
The father is a Scot,
From a time 200 years ago,
I'm afraid that I cannot.

She says she travelled through the stones
While up there picking flowers,
Stayed away for three whole years,
It should have been just hours.

I've been suspected of her murder,
Been a nuisance to the cops,
This story seems a pack of lies,
Now it's time it stops.

But she came back dressed in plaid
And clothes that were not modern
And says that she would not be here,
If there hadn't been Culloden.

She says she's told me everything,
She's not the sort to lie,
And she's promised to forget him,
At least until I die!

I will bring his child up,
I cannot have my own,
I need to have a family
I will not let her down.

The problem is the bedroom,
Claire has become detached,
Her body making promises,
That her mind can't match.

****

A Good Long Ride

From the day that Murtagh found her,
Rescued her from Jack,
In the dimness of that cottage
Where she put my shoulder back.

That long ride sat in front of me
Wedged between my thighs,
Wild brown hair blowing free,
A feast before my eyes,

She's dressed a bit peculiar,
Not for Scottish weather.
How did she end up in her shift
Amongst the Highland heather?

A voice ye canna argue with
Though I would love to try,
She's too classy for a whore,
A face too open for a spy.

She says she is a widow,
She wears a wedding band
A total contradiction
An English stranger in this land.

She's burning through my senses,
Tucked in warm beneath my plaid
Her long back pressed against my chest,
She's driving me quite mad.

I'll keep these pleasant feelings
To myself of course,
But I'll keep enjoying them
Until we both get off this horse.

****

Redcoats

We joined the British Army
To serve the King and fight
A soldiers bed and food and clothes
And whores to spend the night,

Garrisoned in Scotland
It's wet, and cold, and bleak.
We cannot even understand
The strange language that they speak.

The men fight hard like savages,
Their women are all whores,
The children are all bastards,
We'll treat them such I'm sure.

We are here and at the Kings command
We do not need another reason.
To hunt out all the Jacobites
And those disposed to treason.

We take exactly what we want.
And punish who resists.
Fight back and we'll flog you,
Hung up by your wrists.

And when we've raped your women.
And stolen everything,
Remember that we do it all
In the name of our King.

God Save The King!!

The Devils Right Hand Man

Was I really made this way?
Is a mind born dark ?
Was there ever kindness here
Before evil made its mark?

The cloak I made of hatred
Has taken on my soul.
Warped my view of human life
Made misery my goal.

Protected by authority,
Hiding behind rank.
Power is a heady drug
It makes the mind a blank.

Zealous in my actions
I take a twisted pride,
In breaking a mans spirit
The devil is my bride.

I need the screams of torture
For sexual release.
I crave the cries for mercy
To make the torture cease.

For I can break you always
I can invade your mind.
In your sleeping hours I'll haunt you
No peace from me you find.

And when I've taken everything,
When I own your soul,
When no arms can comfort you,
When death becomes your goal.

I will be there waiting,
Smiling – whip in hand
To rob you of your final sleep,
The Devils right hand man.

****

The first visit

My god the place was so remote
It took an age to find,
A peaceful, ordered visit
Not what we had in mind.

The Laird was plainly not at home,
Greeted by his daughter
A Bonnie girl, with fiery eyes
A lamb come to the slaughter.

Let's have some entertainment.
While the men load up the cart.
Humiliate the lassie
Before we make a start.

He strode into the dooryard,
Hate blazed from every pore!
Trying to save his sister
Before I hurt her more.

He was really more my type,
A rare specimen of flesh,
He would be a challenge
And my soul he would enmesh.

Tied up in the gateway
I marked his virgin skin.
With intent of further punishment.
That I would soon begin.

She spat at me with venom
She kicked me and she fought,
Then laughed at me, and taunted
She emasculated thought.

Without the stimulus of fear
The screams that will entreat.
The more I tried the more she laughed.
Humiliation was complete

She could not know, that I had planned
A vengeance like no other.
The deepest darkest pit of hell,
Where I would break her brother.

****

Flogging

He walked in chains up to the post
Stripped down to the waist.
The welts still raw from last time
Wounds dressed with charcoal paste.

A further hundred lashes
Laid upon the last.
Who could bear to see their son
Arms braced, hung from that mast.

The crowd looked on in silence
As punishment was read.
And Captain Black Jack Randall
Took the Cat instead.

This was something personal
Tween my son and Captain Jack
His eyes were gleaming
As he laid the lash on Jamie's back.

I counted strokes inside my head
Flesh and blood were flowing.
He could not break this son of mine
Despite the pain now showing.

He did not cry for mercy,
He would not give an inch,
The Captain lost composure,
But Jamie would not flinch.

My heart was pounding wildly
As Jack flogged him to the bone
A blinding headache felled me
I fell dead as a stone.

My spirit lives with Jamie
I have his back ye ken
My big braw stubborn Fraser lad
Is never giving in.

****

Alex Macgregors Bible

When I was rescued from Fort William
All those years ago,
I'd made a promise to myself,
It's one I have let go.

After Randall flogged me,
The Doctor came to call
Gave me a small bible,
It's owner dead – recall.

He was only eighteen
When Randall tried his case,
The lad then went and hanged himself,
The shame would not erase.

It's still inside my sporran
With all my precious things,
The moles foot, and the blade and bow
And Sawney and some string.

I promised to return it
After Jack was dead,
But life took me another way,
To the colonies instead.

I must add him to my list,
Of lost ones that I pray for,
Young Alex, know, your bible
Helped me live, just one day more.

****

My Godfather

He's always been there with me
Since I was a lad,
Looked out for me and watched my back.
The Da I never had.

Sworn to give his life for mine
His loyalty unswerving.
I know that he can read my mind
In a way which is unnerving.

Murtagh Fitzgibbons Fraser
Is part of my blood
And I will keep an eye on him
When no others think I should.

Tis only right that I should protect
The one who protects me.
As long as I have air to breathe
That is how it will be.

But he is a man who will go his way
Until my time of need.
And when our path diverges
I wish him god speed.

For I am grown and my life now
Has different needs to his
But he always has a place in me
And I a place in his.

I hope I never see him waste his life
On another pointless cause
Fighting for what he believes is right
He is too old for wars.

When at last I have a home
And Claire is by my side
I pray Murtagh stands before my fire
Warming his backside.

****

Machiavellian!

War Chief of Clan Mackenzie
Brother to the Laird,
A man of strong convictions
We've never seen him scared.

His loyalty is to Scotland first
A Jacobite fanatic.
When called to order by his Laird
He is not diplomatic.

Raising money for the Bonnie Prince,
And the King across the water.
To rid Scotland of the English
He will not give them quarter.

He thinks the world of Jamie
But will use him to his ends.
His nephew has the Clans respect
And Dougals running out of friends.

He is an old school warrior
He won't play by the rules,
Doesn't see the need for drilling
Thinks the English fools.

He can show a deal of kindness
But there's always a price to pay.
If he could, he'd marry Claire
But Jamie's in the way

At Preston pans a hero
And a villain in one day.
He won't stop once his blood is up
It's red mist all the way.

He cannot see the cause is lost
Believes the Scots can win.
Can't see the Bonnie Prince a fool
Won't think of giving in.

He will be killed by Jamie
He overhears a plot
To poison his dear Bonnie Prince
Someone must die on the spot.

An arch manipulator,
He plots and schemes and plans.
Dear old Machiavelli
Would be so proud of this man.

****

Angus Mhor

Angus Mhor – Big Angus
But on TV I'm not large.
I'm kind of like a terrier.
I growl a lot, then charge.

I'm a Clansman, a Mackenzie
And with my wingman Rupert
We live at Castle Leoch
And travel round with Dougal.

If I want a fight, I'll start one
I'm an expert with a knife.
I wasn't really fussed on Claire,
When she became Jamie's wife.

She's not like Scottish women,
She'll no do as she's told,
She'll get in serious trouble here
Before she gets too old.

Jamie's got his hands full
With his feisty English wife.
If he doesna get a grip on her.
He may just lose his life.

He needs to have a wee word,
Remind her of her place.
To rescue her is not our job.
We've enough upon our plates.

Sort yer wife out Jamie,
In the Scottish way
Spare the strap and spoil the wife.
Dougals' men would say.

****

Mor of Angus (see what I did) I

I never met a smaller man,
Who thought himself sae big,
He is na much tae look at,
But he doesna give a fig,

He's handsome, rugged, charming
And suave a proper gent,
A winner with the ladies,
It's all in his mind ye ken!

He cannae help his temper,
It comes from being small,
The urge tae get his weapon out,
If any cause should call!

He's never had to use his sword,
If he's gonna tak yer life
He doesna care how big ye are,
He'll always use his knife.

He's really a wee gobshite,
No more brains than he has teeth,
But wee Angus has a heart of gold
Hiding underneath.

****

Rupert Thomas Alexander Mackenzie

Jamie had a choice ye ken
She coulda married me.
Yon red haird loon coulda said no
To the bride to be.

But I dinna think she'd gang fer me
I'm really no her thing,
A bit more rough and ready – ye ken.
Than the lad that bought the ring.

He'd already gone all gooey eed
Since when she fixed his arm.
She's handy with the stitches ay
And she doesna try to harm.

She does all that by accident,
She doesna have tae try
Keepin them safe's a full time job
But ye ken that by and by.

So me and my wee Angus
May chaff her – here and there.
But we'd both lay our lives down.
For Jamie and for Claire

****

A Man of Letters

Need a lawyer! Neds the man
To sort your legal papers.
The breadth of his experience
Would give a lady vapours.

A man of education,
By books, and school of life,
From the city to the Highlands,
And he doesn't have a wife!

Qualified in Edinburgh
He is a man of letters,
He also is a Jacobite
Though he's avoided any fetters.

He operates from Leoch
And rides out for the rents
Big buddies with the War Chief!
I think they share a tent!

They have a common purpose,
Money for the cause.
Parade the scars on Jamie's back
To Jacobite applause.

The Lairds rent goes in one bag,
Their collection in another,
They'll be in some hot water,
If it's found by Dougals brother.

Ned will get off lightly,
Talk his way around,
Callum will not banish him,
There are too few lawyers in town.

So if you need your Will writ,
Or treason is your game,
Sell your house? Divorce your wife?
Ned Gowan is the name !

He'll also source a wedding dress
If you're really stuck.
But don't ask where he found it!
"Twas just a stroke of luck

****

The Laird and his wife

A master politician
A shrewd and careful man,
The undisputed figurehead
Of the Mackenzie Clan.

Not a figure to be crossed
He does not suffer fools.
Is swift to issue punishment
To those who break the rules.

The Clan ,is his priority
Before any other cause.
His men at arms will not be sent
To fight Jacobite wars.

Legs crippled and disjointed
He rarely leaves his lair.
His Brother is his War Chief
At his right hand – ever there.

We see little of Letitia
His feisty red haired wife.
Always in the background
But cutting like a knife.

She is a witch it's rumoured
Is know to have her say.
Keeps Callum always on his toes,
Behind the scenes ye Ken

What goes on behind closed doors,
In public they are one
Letitia has her husbands back.
The power behind the throne.

****

A Woman Scorned

Jamie Fraser came to live
At Leoch when I was seven,
I told myself I loved him,
To me he looked like heaven.

Then I thought I'd marry him
But he went away.
When he returned
I knew that he was mine, from that very day.

I'd whiled away the hours,
While I did the chores
Imagining that he was mine.
And the other women, whores.

I told myself small stories
Of imagined married life.
He was Laird of Lallybroch
And I was his wife.

I fantasised and romanced,
Convinced myself twas true.
And when he took my punishment
I knew what I must do.

I made myself available,
I sat where he could see,
But he had eyes only for her
He didn't look at me.

Yes, I let him kiss me
I tried to turn his head
But when the English whore looked at him
I'd just as well be dead.

Cold English whore,
I hated you, even from the start
Jamie Fraser will be mine
You will never have his heart.

And in the end I got him
But life was not all honey.
All I really wanted then,
From my Jamie, was his money.

****

The Full Scottish

Just to set the scene a bit
I shall start the night before
Jamie spent a cold hard night
Asleep outside my door.

The Inn was full of drunkards
And with my safety on his mind
He feared I might have 'visitors'
Of a most unwelcome kind.

At breakfast in the morning
I was sat amongst the men
Porridge doled out for breakfast
But an atmosphere – ye ken

I don't have much Gaelic
Their signals were quite clear
The rabble making phallic signs
And grinning ear to ear.

Angus slammed his bowl down
Then picked up his dirk,
Rupert drew his breath in.
Murtagh gave a smirk.

Even Ned began to look around
For a convenient place to hide
And Dougal quietly nodded.
At Willie by my side.

Angus growled and strolled across,
Said a few words to the lad.
Rammed his head into his porridge
Called him something really bad.

Bodies crashing everywhere!
Plates and fists were thrown
I sat in the corner.
Puzzled and alone.

Bloody Scots! must they pick
A fight at any chance.
More bodies thrown against the wall.
A stamping, kicking dance.

It ended quick as it began
The losers having fled!
I patched up Mackenzie wounds
Bandaged Mackenzie heads.

As guest of the Mackenzie,
They may insult me to be sure.
But god help any other man
Who calls their guest a whore!

I suppose I must be thankful
That the finest of all forces
My red haired, young protector
Had been sent to feed the horses.

****

Planning a Wedding

Dougal thinks I marry lightly,
Believes it's all on paper.
Just wed her, and then bed her
And if she complains then rape her.

But Claire will be mine forever,
And I tell it true,
I will make this day a special one,
If it's the last thing I ever do.

I rummage in my sporran,
I find a special thing,
The front door key to Lallybroch
That will make a ring.

I marry as a Fraser
I am ready – Je suis prest.
I will marry in my Tartan
Not Mackenzie on this day.

And we will be married by a priest
In the papist way
And in a church – before God
And the blood oath we must say.

My bride must also have a dress,
Something verra fine,
to suit the Lady Lallybroch
That she'll be will be when she is mine.

And so I laid my conditions down,
To wed my Sassenach
A marriage till we both should die
There would be no turning back.

****

Second time Around

It was a formal document
Writ with quill and ink.
Sat on a log I read it.
And took down a stiff drink.

But I already had a husband,
Though he was not yet born,
How could I take another one.
Tomorrow in the morn.

The groom did not seem worried
In fact he seemed quite sure.
It didn't seem to phase him.
That I'd done it all before.

I stamped my feet a little.
And had another drink.
I think I drank the bottle
While I had a think.

It wasn't really bigamy
Franks time was not yet due
Was Jamie then, my first husband.
Had he just jumped the queue!

I did get very drunk that day,
I don't remember night.
I woke up with a steaming head.
And looking quite a fright.

But someone had produced a dress
And a very charming ring.
A church bedecked with candles
And a priest to do his thing.

And oh my when I saw the groom
Dressed in highland splendour.
I had a feeling that the wedding night
Would see my heart surrender.

****

The Wedding Night

There was a certain atmosphere
In the room above the Inn,
The all male wedding party
Were making quite a din,

Despite the lack of planning,
There was really quite a spread
The wine and whisky flowing,
Washing down the meat and bread.

This wasn't my first wedding night,
But the last was much more quiet,
Without the punctuation,
Of Clansmen fit to riot,

I'd shed the dress, kicked off my shoes,
And sat there in my stays
Combing out my pinned up hair,
Planning what to say.

Dougal wanted witnesses,
To be sure we didn't cheat
Would Rupert and – hell -Angus
Want a front row seat!

My thoughts were interrupted ,
I pulled out of my gloom,
The door was softly opened,
To admit – the groom.

We talked and drank into the night,
I asked a lot of questions,
We learned of each other's families.
Discussed the men's suggestions.

And when we finally got to bed,
To make it all official,
The depth of his emotion
Was far from superficial.

Suffice to say my virgin groom
Proved to be quite a scholar
And by the time the sun came up
He'd learned how to make me holler!

✳✳✳✳

Gaberlunzie

All men have a history,
Some have more than most,
A past which colours all their life.
About which they do not boast.

An educated person,
In Latin and in Greek,
A passer on of messages
Though he cannot speak.

Reduced to a beggar,
And living off the land,
He wanders through the parishes,
Tokens in his hand,

This little gaberlunzie,
Is always in the know,
He gathers information,
Passes it to and fro.

His hands enact his message
Conversation done in mime
With nods and winks, and grunts and groans,
And in Gaelic half the time.

Redcoats do not trouble him,
They cannot understand,
The secrets he is carrying
In the waving of his hands,

If you've lost somebody,
Or are searching for a friend,
Huw Munro will find him,
Loyal to the end.

****

Locked in time

Locked in time forever,
Frozen in it's world.
It's beauty now imprisoned,
Hovering wings now stilled.

Viewed as through a window,
Never to be freed,
A gift for such a couple,
A rarity indeed.

The properties of Amber
Push back the mists of time.
An ancient medication
To tranquillise the mind.

And it survived Culloden.
A memory of the lost.
Now preserved behind a glass
Not in the April frost.

Our wedding gift from Huw Munro,
His more than precious find.
A gift from one with nothing
But an educated mind.

****

85

Self Defence

I'd only learned the day before,
How to use a knife,
The best way to stick it in
Ways to take a life,

I'd watched in stunned amazement,
How the Clansmen used their tools,
Proficient all with sword and dirk
They do not suffer fools.

Even Ned the lawyer,
Carries his own blade
A small knife – a sghian dhu
Specially made.

They taught me to defend myself,
It was a masterclass,
But didn't think I'd use it.
Quite so bloody fast.

The rolling Scottish hillside,
The very place to sneak
To fulfil your urges,
When you haven't done all week.

Deserting Redcoat soldiers,
Caught us in the act.
Looking down a pistol,
An edifying fact.

Jamie held at gunpoint,
To watch them do the deed.
He stank worse than a sewer
The lowest of his breed!

I waited for the moment,
When he could not backtrack.
With all the strength that I could muster
I stabbed him in the back,

I heard the gun, I saw the blood,
I felt his life force leave,
Stuck underneath his body,
For Jamie to retrieve.

If you venture up the hillside.
In your hour of need,
Don't forget to take your knife
These are dangerous times indeed!

When you are in flagrante,
Even with your wife,
Keep one eye o'er yer shoulder,
Or you may risk your life !!

****

A rare old sodomite

More faces than the Town Hall Clock,
In league with Black Jack Randall.
A friend of Clan Mackenzie
And not averse to scandal.

He plays his cards close to his chest,
Changing with the wind.
You'll never know which side he's on
He likes to change his mind.

Flushing out the Jacobites,
But financing their advance,
He runs with hare and hunts with hounds
And leads all a merry dance.

Resplendent dressed in silks and wig
He likes to drink and gamble.
Owes money to the worst of folk
And lies without preamble.

A man of quite some influence,
He can get you heard.
But would you trust this fickle man
He'd hang you with a word.

The devious Duke of Sandringham
Knows what he enjoys.
His appetite is rampant,
For good looking teenage boys

This upper class old sodomite
Expects his quid pro quo.
Would he get Jamie pardoned
He'd want something back we know

That double dealing bastard
Will meet a fitting end,
Beheaded in his kitchen
By Murtagh our good friend.

****

Drama in the hall

Come quick lass – your wanted.
Come quick to the hall!
Fetch one of your potions
Or – better fetch them all !

Dougal has gone fighting drunk
His wife at home is deid.
On the quiet he blames himself.
He's drunk off his heid.

There was Dougal, sword in hand.
Trashing up the place
Screaming like a banshee.
Tears running down his face.

He'll thrash the ears off anyone
Trying to get near.
Wee Angus was the only one
Not showing any fear.

I loaded up the bottle.
With laudanum ,I think
I'll give it to wee Angus
To try and make him drink.

Wee Angus raised the bottle high
And offered it to his Chief
They drank a toast to Maura
We all sighed with relief.

As the big War Chief Mackenzie
Collapsed upon the floor
And with Clansmen holding arms and legs
Was carried out the door.

Drop him and I'll have yer balls!
The Lairds voice was a warning.
Put the drunken sot to bed
I'll see him in the morning!

****

Cranesmuir

Jamie warned me not to,
But I had to go.
The note from Geilis called me,
The rest I think you know.

She'd always walked a fine line
Between darkness and the light.
I knew she'd killed her husband
With Cyanide that night.

Nothing to protect her
From the anger of the Laird
Dougal gone to exile – with my Jamie.
I was scared.

The wardens came for both of us,
And Laoghaire came to gloat.
I knew then it wasn't Geilis
Who sent that bloody note.

Tried by the Church as witches,
I knew that we'd be burned.
Ned Gowan did his very best
But then the tables turned.

Burn the Witch, Skelp her!
Take them to pyre.
Burn the Witch! Burn the Witch!
The most painful death is fire.

I will dance upon your ashes,
Laoghaire screamed in glee.
As they flogged me with that strap,
She was all that I could see.

Then through the baying of the crowd,
Cutting like a knife.
I heard my Jamie shouting.
He'd come to claim his wife!

****

The Witch

I am a Scottish Nationalist
Fanatic for the cause.
An independent Scotland
Let's hear some applause.

To go back where it started,
With the Bonnie Prince.
My mission to change history
No matter what the price.

So in 1968, I travelled back in time
To try and aid the Jacobites
Put our King back on the throne.
The Scots were doomed, their cause would fail
If they fought for it alone.

Adept at making potions,
A gossip and a bitch.
No wonder all the local folk
Thought I was a witch.

The War Chief of Clan Mackenzie
Took me to his bed
His life devoted to the cause
A love that we both shared.

I didn't burn at Cranesmuir
I was big with child
My dearest darling Dougal
Went a trifle wild.

They burned another woman
That morning on the square.
She had died already
It made sure I wasn't there.

My little boy was fostered out
At least to a Mackenzie.
Dougal sent to exile
His brother in a frenzy.

And I skipped off across the sea
And settled in Jamaica.
Bathed in blood and virgin boys.
They now call me the Bakra

I will fulfil the prophecy
that the last of Lovats line
Will rule over Scotland
I will have what's mine

Claire was here for something
But she doesn't yet know why
Her child with Jamie Fraser
Really has to die.

But it all comes to nothing
I'll die in that dark cave
In 200yrs they will find my bones
And think I was a slave.

****

Jenny Murray

My brother came home with a wife
A Sassenach for sure.
He started well, upsetting me.
Calling me a whore.

Of consorting with a redcoat
Of having Black Jacks child
Didn't know I'd married Ian Mor
Thought I'd been defiled.

Strutted back into the house
Saying that I lied.
I've been in charge since he ran off
Since our father died.

His wife is quite a strange one
She clearly loves him dear.
But has no family and no history.
I find that really queer.

I will have the truth from him
Before he moves back tween these walls
And if he's telling lies to me
I shall have him by his balls.

Brother or no brother
He need not expect
That strutting in and playing Laird
Will earn him my respect.

I want him to be happy,
To settle here with me,
Without a price upon his head.
And most of all be free.

There'd been all sorts of stories
Came from Leoch, of his wife.
She'd best not hurt my brother.
For him I'd give my life.

She appeared out of nowhere.
Some believe she is a witch,
Others that she is a spy
I will find out which is which.

My brother clearly loves her,
And I will play along.
Until the day she crosses me
And does my brother wrong.

****

Ian Mor

I was Jamie's childhood friend,
We shared everything
The scrapes, the pranks, the thrashings
God that strap could sting.

We were a team together
I always had his right,
Protecting of his weaker side,
If he has one in a fight.

We fought in France together
Then I lost my leg,
I returned to Scotland
Walking with a peg.

I'd always loved his sister
Jenny was my lass,
Despite the rumours Dougal spread.
A marriage came to pass.

Now the red heid eejits back,
Jumping to conclusions
I think I'll play along before
I shatter his illusions,

There's a way to handle Frasers
And Claire had best learn quick,
When they get to boiling point
Don't poke them with yer stick.

Ye'd best let them get on with it,
They'll shout and curse a bit,
Remove all deadly weapons,
Or someone might get hit.

And when this pair have trashed the house
Done screaming through the halls,
If Jenny really wants to talk.
She'll grab him by his balls.

****

The Laird has a Hangover

My mouth was like the desert
Head pounding fit to burst,
I haven't had a morning
When I woke up feeling worse.

I'd been welcomed by the tenants
Drunk a dram or ten
Given most an ease of rent,
I am the Laird ye ken!

Breakfast was a challenge,
I was feeling in a state,
My stomach started heaving
At the kipper on my plate.

I don't need a herbal cure,
My head begins to pound,
Don't give me one hair of the dog.
I could drink the whole damn hound.

****

Fixing the Mill

Little things remembered
Small details in your mind
Things that you can laugh at now
That time has them behind.

The day I went to fix the mill
And redcoats came a riding
One had to be a millers son
And I was in the water hiding.

He came striding to the mill wheel
And gave it a good shake.
I was in the water weed
Hiding like a snake

I held my breath for ever!
He would not go away.
The cold was doing things to me
I remember to this day.

I pushed the wheel from underneath,
The gears began to bite.
And hung my fathers flannel drawers,
On the paddles in full sight.

The redcoats rode off on their way.
They'd be back later - maybe
I was in the millpond,
As naked as a baby.

As I emerged – granny McNab
Was sitting on the grass.
Skirts arranged around her.
Laughing at my arse.

I would have blushed, had I not been blue
I tried to hide my tackle
That rare old crone stared back at me
And then began to cackle.

Young Rabbie to be a stable boy?
She asked in wily tones
Grinning ,and her toothless laugh
Shaking her old bones.

Claire was sat beside her
Laughing fit to burst!
I'd give grannie anything.
But I'd have my sark back first.

Caught at a disadvantage
She pushed it to the hilt,
It's hard not to grant a favour,
When she's sitting on yer kilt

****

A Visit from the Watch

The Watch rode into Lallybroch,
As though they owned the place,
I think they were a bit surprised,
   By the look upon my face.

They wanted food and lodging,
   As promised them, by Jenny,
   Like as not they'd eat a lot,
   And then not pay a penny.

A pistol stuck right up my nose
   I'll not give them a meg,
   We do not pay protection,
   And I'm not about to beg.

   Horrocks is a dead man,
   A red coat, who deserted.
He for one will not be missed,
With the devil he has flirted.

I ken they've planned to rob the rents
      To carry out his plan
With Horrocks gone, they won't complain
   If I am now their man.

   We ended up in Wentworth,
   In shackles with the rest
   This time for the gibbet.
Not the flogging post I guessed.

McQuarrie full of bluster,
With that rope around his neck,
He did not get a nice clean drop,
And I knew I was next.

****

On the Run

Of all the foolish things I did
To pacify McQuarry,
When we rode out from Lallybroch
I'd a feeling I'd be sorry.

The ambush set by Horrocks
Wasn't in his plan.
Redcoats swarmed all over us.
We'd be killed down to a man.

All were dead but he and I
We're off again to jail
I must escape or face the rope.
This time I cannot fail.

I threw myself down off the cart,
Into the swollen river,
Icy water chilled my bones,
The current made me shiver.

Nowhere now was safe for me,
living rough, without a hope,
On the run, a wanted man,
Next stop was the rope.

I got the message that they sent,
With their idiots invention.
A healer and a dancing loon.
Attracting my attention.

I did go to see their show,
But the Gypsy stole her song
They shipped me off to Wentworth.
Shopped to the RedCoats all along.

With all the poor, decrepit souls,
I wait without a friend.
As one by one at point of gun,
They dance at the ropes end.

The noose is placed around my neck,
Before I take the drop,
A voice booms out across the yard.
It's Randall, shouting stop!

He's for Interrogation,
Take him to a cell!
I knew that I was entering
his special form of Hell.

Unconscious in the darkness
I'm sure I heard, but how,
The welcome voice of Murtagh,
And the lowing of a cow.

✳✳✳✳

The Aftermath

Ye cannae take these thoughts away,
Ye cannae ease my mind,
He's living there both night and day,
Sees through my eyes - I'm blind.

Mend my hand and heal my scars,
Salve me where he burned,
I cannot sleep for seeing him,
Pain cannot be un learned.

I shut my eyes and long dark hair
Falls across my chest.
I convince myself that it is Claire
But the image doesn't rest.

The cloying smell of lavender,
Hovers in the air.
Her face is gone, and he is back
I know that she's not there.

My hands reach out to grab his throat,
I'd kill him with one squeeze.
But pain invades my every move,
It brings me to my knees.

You cannot feed me happiness,
I cannot drink peace,
You cannot stitch back hands of time,
You cannot kill the beast.

My lips cannot caress you,
Without feeling of revulsion,
I hurt inside with things he did
There is nothing but repulsion.

He broke my mind of happiness
He broke my body too.
He broke the only thing I love
I cannot be a man to you.

****

A Hot Bath.

A cave beneath the monastery
Dark as blessed night,
A hot spring fills a pitch black lake.
Stars provide the only light.

I floated in the darkness,
Feeling my self heal,
Warmth invaded all my scars,
I began once more to feel.

Water washed right through my soul,
I felt the pain depart,
Maybe it could heal us both,
Of sorrows to our hearts.

I thought of all she'd said and done,
Her selfless act of courage.
Her desperate plea that she could heal,
My mind and then our marriage.

I will bring her to this sacred place.
Hold her in my arms.
Let the water do it's work,
Let the heat work all it's charms.

We need to find connection,
We need to find a path,
And I know what she misses most.
Claire loves a good hot bath.

****

A Rough Crossing

Scotland is not safe for us,
They'll not take this lying down,
Breaking out of Wentworth,
An assault against the Crown.

I have family in France,
We might be in position,
To try and stop the Bonnie Prince,
That now would be our mission.

Ships are coffins on the sea,
But on one I must bide,
I ken I'll spend the next few days,
Puking o'er the side.

Throwing up with broken ribs,
Is a painful and most grieving.
So they forced laudanum down my throat
To try and stop me heaving.

Now In France on solid ground,
A new future we seek,
Put me to bed sweet Sassenach
I could sleep for a week.

****

The Bonnie Prince

Charles Edward Stuart
What were people thinking!
To put you on the Scottish throne,
They must have been drinking.

Brought up an Italian,
Pampered by the pope.
You'd never been to Scotland.
You never had a hope.

You misled the Highland Clansmen,
You misled your own advisors,
An army can't be armed and fed
With money spent like misers.

You thought yourself a leader,
You tried to look the part,
Believed the ones that flattered you,
It was all doomed from the start.

Fortunate in your victories
Your army gave their all.
The English learned their lessons.
God couldn't stop your fall.

God will not grant you victory
On that moor so wet and sodden.
God will not save the Scottish Clans
At the Battle of Culloden

****

Parisian to the core

When I was a still a child
I made a big mistake.
I stole something from a Scotsman
A little wooden snake.

Of very little value
To anyone but him.
I stole it from his sporran
And he didn't feel a thing.

It changed my life forever,
That's when I met milord.
For that is what I called him
When my future he assured.

He took me from the brothel
I was born there, no excuse
And he paid me to steal for him
My talent put to use.

He vowed he would look after me
If I lost a hand,
Or any other body part
In the service of his land.

And I am married his daughter
No longer a French rake
Maybe stealing Sawny
Was not such a mistake.

For milord adopted me.
When we married by the sea
Fergus Claudel Fraser.
I have his name and family.

****

Eat a Healthy Breakfast

King Louis had a problem,
In pain without a doubt,
Too much rich food going in,
Nothing would come out.

He strained, and cursed and sweated,
Then a Scot made a suggestion,
Eat porridge for yer breakfast sire,
It will aid digestion.

Peasant food, I could not!
It's for commoners – not I,
You would not have this problem,
If you'd just give it a try.

The humble oat, for breakfast
Is the Scottish meal of choice,
Eat yer porridge up there lad,
The Scots say with one voice!

Fills ye every morning,
Keeps ye warm as well,
And regular as clockwork,
And no constipation hell !!

****

Mysterious French apothecary,
Perceptive and alert,
His shop is full of remedies
Though some of them are dirt.

We do not know much of him,
Though he moves amongst Royalty,
He dabbles in the dark arts
That is the reality.

Mainly he is un demoniste blanc,
His powers are for healing.
His aura blue, the same as Claire.
They have the same good feeling.

Where he ever came from,
We really do not know,
Older than very time itself,
Traveller ? That may be so.

He saves Claire's life, by laying hands,
He brings her out of fever
But then falls foul of St Germaine
The Count is a deceiver.

Before the King, Claire must judge
Who uses those dark powers
By sleight of hand the Master,
Puts an end to the Counts living hours,

Banished then from all of France
He leaves without a trace.
Is he in some other time?
Travelled to another place?

****

Idle Hands

An endless round of pointlessness
Of gossip and taking tea,
Is this all I can look forward to,
Here in gay Paree!

These vapid Parisienne women
Are really not my scene.
Especially when I'm turning
Morning sickness green.

I feel like I'm abandoned,
With just this house to run,
Sitting in my gilded cage,
While he has all the fun!

He won't be very happy,
But I'm going to volunteer,
As a healer in the Hospital,
Now that's a good idea.

If he can stay out late at night
Talking politics and treason
At least I'll occupy my day.
And give my life a reason.

Working late and going home
With tales of suppurations
Stitching wounds, and bandaging
And nasty amputations.

Well it went down like a lead balloon,
It nearly wrecked our marriage,
Should have listened to what Murtagh said,
When we got into the carriage.

****

Loss of Faith

The bright new hope, I'd given him
Of his flesh, and bone
Lay now cold beneath the ground,
Underneath that stone.

Had I done wrong, to go to work,
Would it have been best,
To sit at home, and incubate,
And just forget the rest.

And he would play the blame game too,
A great regret he'd feel
A dual, then arrested.
Locked in the Bastille,

He'll think of her at some odd hour,
And wonder what she'd be,
His lost little daughter,
Who looked so much like Bree.

I counted her fingers, and her toes
They numbered four times five.
My baby was born perfect
Just too small to survive

She would have been a beauty,
I could see it, latent there,
Pale white skin, bright blue eyes
And a fuzz of bright red hair.

The things we lost in Paris,
That louche deceitful place,
Our Honour and integrity,
And most of all our faith.

****

The Old Fox

When trying to raise an army,
You'll look anywhere for troops,
That wily man my grand sire
Would make us jump through hoops.

Lord Lovat, has trained fighting men,
The soldiers of his Clan,
But first we must do business
With this double dealing man.

There is always an agenda
A benefit to him,
To get him to declare his hand,
My chances are quite slim.

What is the bastard up to,
My brain is in a frenzy,
Why would he take it on himself,
To call up The Mackenzie.

So here's the deal before me,
I hand him back my land,
Then I have his fighting men
And he calls out his Clan.

Or he sides with Callum
And claims neutrality
Claims he's loyal to King George,
If we lose, he is Scot free.

This game of cards continues,
His son will call the men,
Claire has had a hand in that,
She's helpful, now and then.

That masterful old bastard,
Has spun it to his ends,
Claims loyalty to both sides,
With George and Charles ye ken.

History will play out,
And when we're taking stock,
The Old Fox Simon Fraser
Dies on the chopping block.

****

Carryarick

I was just sixteen years old
When I met Red Jamie Fraser,
A wanted man, a Jacobite,
And I not quite a soldier.

I saw him in the dark by chance,
Pissing up against a wall
I thought I'd try and cut his throat
Boy was I a fool.

Although his hands were busy,
As I raised my knife
Swift as a snake he seized my arm,
And held me like a vice.

He said he wouldn't kill me,
And then he warmed the knife.
He held the red end to my face.
And then I met — his wife.

She played the hostage English girl
Kept there by Scots force.
Willing to give her honour up,
To save my sorry arse.

And so I told them everything,
I spilled my cowardly guts.
Of cannon, troops and cavalry
It really was quite nuts.

I swore that as he spared my life,
I would not kill him now,
But held a debt of honour
It would get paid – and how.

They took me to the woodland,
And tied me to a tree,
They found me there at daybreak,
My own comrades set me free.

That night at Carryarick
A naïve callow English Lord.
Vowed to kill a Scotsman
Destined to meet abroad.

A man who never breaks his word,
Who commands a great respect,
A loyal friend, you'd trust with life
Is not what you expect.

They told us Scots were savages.
Their habits were barbaric,
But I met a gentleman
That night at Carryarick.

****

PrestonPans

We Scots had the high ground.
Could see across the bog
The rows and rows of British tents,
Appearing through the fog.

Between us yards of marshy ground,
And all were at a loss,
There was no way, on this fine day,
That we could get across.

He rode out into no mans land,
A brave man or a fool,
Out of the range of musket fire,
He broke every rule.

To test the ground for soundness,
Or sink hock deep in mire
To Scottish cheers and war cry's,
He drew the musket fire.

Only one man for the job,
The War Chief of Mackenzie,
Rode out to taunt the British
To whip them to a frenzy.

There was no path across that bog,
But one would lead us round,
At dawn we would surprise them,
For victory we were bound.

We won the day at Preston Pans,
Not many men were lost.
Except for brave wee Angus,
Blown up by cannon shot.

We miss his clarty attitude,
His wicked sense of fun,
Rupert will miss him most of all,
Their two is now a one.

****

Culloden - Jamie's Story

I watched my life go safely
Through a granite ring of stone.
I galloped to Culloden field
To face my fate alone

A murderer of Dougal,
A traitor to the Crown,
A cause I knew would soon be lost
Brave warriors all mown down.

A leader still amongst my men
I lined up on that field
Prepared to charge the British guns.
The Bonnie Prince won't yield.

And so began the Highland charge,
We heard the muskets rattle,
The cannon blast, the smell of death
The chaos of the battle.

It lasted but an hour
Of volleys and of shots,
Red coated soldiers waded in
The bodies of the Scots.

A flash of red a horse of black
I saw him through the fog
Captain Black Jack Randall
Riding 'cross the bog.

Pulled from his horse
My eyes met his – his death was writ in stone
My sword met his – neither one
Of us would die alone.

I felt the steel slice up my leg,
My strength was nearly gone
I thrust my dirk into his guts
His life on earth was done.

We fell together to the the ground
Trapped in deaths embrace
I heard him moan 'I love you – Claire
As tears streamed down his face.

I lay there underneath his corpse,
The heather neath my head.
Eyes sealed shut with crusted blood
I knew I should be dead.

I saw her walking 'cross the moor
A cloud of Bonnie hair
She called my name – she came to me
My soul called out for – Claire

Dragged from the moor ,and to a farm
Bedraggled, starving, wounded
Waiting for the red coats
We knew we would be hounded.

Each Clansman proudly gave his name,
Was added to the roll.
And stood to meet that musket ball
That added to deaths toll.

I gave them then my name in full
And prayed for absolution.
And for a second time a man in red
Stopped my execution.

✳✳✳✳

Half a life

Half a life for twenty years
A bargain made in haste.
To not discuss my darkest hours
To let my talents waste.

I promised one I would stay safe
The other, I'd move on.
It broke my heart to leave my love
The wrong side of that stone.

Returning to my rightful time
Carrying his child.
How to explain my absence
She's mad – they say with smiles.

For twenty years I've missed him,
More with every day.
An aching deep within my soul
It will not go away.

Sometimes I feel him touch me
Watching as I sleep,
Not to dream he's with me
Is a promise I can't keep.

I'll search the books in secret,
I really need to know,
Does he lie dead at Culloden
Underneath the snow

How do I tell our daughter,
What will seem quite mad,
Her unknown Scottish heritage
The truth about her dad.

Now Frank is gone.
There are no ties, to this time, so at last
I can tell our daughter, her history
And my past.

For twenty years I've mourned him,
Pretended life was fine.
And if by chance he's still alive
I will go back to his time.

****

Ian the Wanderer

Redcoats raided Lallybroch
The day that I was born.
They'd heard the sound of gunfire
From the farm that very morn.

I was in my uncle Jamie's arms,
Him a wanted man ye ken,
His face the first I ever saw,
I think we bonded then.

My name is Ian Murray
They named me for my da.
But I'm more like my uncle
I am Fraser to the core.

My ma just wants to keep me close,
I'm the youngest of her flock,
She thinks I'll stay upon the farm
With Da and be his rock.

I want to go adventuring
I've grown up , I'm not a child
Ma would keep me on her apron strings
It's driving me quite wild.

I've run away to Uncle Jamie
He's had to take me back,
And then I get a thrashing
My arse is blue and black.

He followed to Jamaica
When I was kidnapped by a ship,
To take me back home to ma
If I survived the trip.

If I hadna been kidnapped
There would be no Frasers Ridge,
We would na have left Scotland
I think they're glad we did.

When I stayed with the Indians
It made me the man I am
I've learned to live a simple life
I am a simple man.

Highlander and Mohawk
I had an Indian wife,
When I had to leave her,
It was the worst time of my life.

I'm tied to Uncle Jamie
With him I always have a home.
He is the star which guides me
Wherever I should roam.

****

The Dun Bonnet

My leg was so infected
I thought that I should die,
Fever ravaged through me
I was hot enough to fry.

How Jenny saved my wounded leg,
Determined, as she's small
There was boiling water,
And a knife as I recall.

She cut the dead flesh from my leg
And boiled it to the bone,
The pain enough to kill me,
I faced it all alone.

With RedCoats still out hunting
To round up Charlie's men,
The house was not a home to me,
I was living rough again.

A cave became my bedroom,
I hunted for my keep
A feral man with wild red hair.
In the forest deep.

The village made a hero,
Who wore a hat of brown
To cover up his bright red hair,
Who fought against the Crown.

Red Jamie, had once been their Laird.
But loyalties were torn,
On the broadsheets rife in every town
The Dun Bonnet was born.

No man can survive that way
Live in constant danger
Hunted like a rabid dog
To his family a stranger.

Jenny took the British gold
I made her turn me in
It got the Red Coats off their back
But She'll no forgive ye ken.
.
The British had stopped hanging.
So it's Prison for my crime.
Ardsmuir Is a hell on earth,
In anybody's time.

****

Ardsmuir Prison to Helwater

He would not shoot me at Culloden
Did not expect me to survive
The journey back to Lallybroch
Would not see me alive.

My family pulled me from that cart,
A shadow of a man.
A wounded leg, a shattered heart,
A very wounded mind.

And still the English hunted us,
Survivors from that day.
They hounded us from hearth and home,
They would not go away.

I became a hermit,
hiding in a cave.
Creeping out when all was safe,
The stories said - "twas brave!

How do you tell the ones you love,
That half of you is gone,
That life is just a passing time,
Not worth the carrying on.

Six years spent inside that cave,
A prison made of stone.
Of my own construction
So I could be alone.

Still a price upon my head,
And no food in their larder.
The family starved times were hard,
The red coats made it harder.

I made them give my freedom up,
If freedom it was really,
The money taken from the Crown
Would feed my kinfolk freely.

Fettered - sent to Ardsmuir,
A hellhole of a prison.
The only man they kept in chains
They feared me for a reason.

A change of Governor came around
A fortuitous day.
To renew an old acquaintance
With Major Lord John Grey.

I dined often with the Major,
We played a lot of chess,
His company was sociable
I wouldn't expect less.

We traded information,
Improved the prisoners lot.
His brother was the bastard
Who wouldn't have me shot.

He needed my assistance
To search for Frenchman's gold.
To translate from the Gaelic
The stories that were told.

And when they closed the Prison,
And sent my men across the water,
For reasons of his own.
Lord John paroled me to Helwater.

****

Life at Ardsmuir

Herded in like cattle
Many to a cell,
A days hard work on little food
The Scottish form of hell.

Few here with the will to fight
We were already beaten
Culloden ripped the soul from us.
The bit the rats hadna eaten.

They searched the cells for tartan,
A reminder still for some
Stuffed into the cracks in walls.
A tiny scrap of home.

The guards had cause to fear me
I'd been sentenced twice to die.
As murderer and traitor.
Though there were reasons why.

The only man they kept in chains
With nothing left to lose.
I'd kill most of them with just one hand.
If my anger was let loose.

Clansmen need a leader,
They found me work to do
Red Jamie, The Dun Bonnet.
They Christened me Mac Dubh.

So I tried to make things better
To hunt for food and that.
Blankets, greens and medicine
But they didn't want the cat.

So we rebuilt the prison.
And then they moved us on
Indentured to the colonies
Far away from home.

But they would not send me with them
My crimes deserved no quarter.
They paroled me as a servant.
And sent me to Helwater.

"Twas Lord John Grey arranged it
Only later could I tell.
It was a favour to the only friend
The good Lord found in Hell.

****

To Helwater and Back

Arriving at Helwater
Indentured as a groom
To serve the Lord Dunsany,
At least there's loads of room.

His Lordship is a fair man,
He treats his staff alright,
But his wife Lady Dunsany
Hates all Jacobites.

Not known by my proper name,
I am now known as Mac.
It's better here than Ardsmuir,
With sunshine on my back.

His Lordship has two daughters,
The eldest one Geneva,
Spoiled, petulant and headstrong
She's a schemer and deceiver.

Betrothed to the Earl of Ellesmere
Whose older than her father.
She demands I take her off to bed
Because it's me she'd rather.

She threatens me with prison,
She threatens all my kin,
She'll tell her mother I'm Red Jamie.
God knows what she'd make of him.

So I climb in through the window,
And creep along the halls,
For just the one night only
She's got me by the balls.

She visits some months later,
I hand her off the carriage,
She's clearly been up the duff
Since early in her marriage.

A boy is born, his mother dies
The Earl calls him a bastard!
He calls his teenage wife a whore
Her bed he hadn't mastered.

He threatens then to kill the boy
I'm called to stop the trouble.
I end up shooting the old Earl
The child could be my double.

It's all hushed up and swept away
Under an English rug.
Misadventure says the coroner
And dismisses with a shrug.

Six years on I'm pardoned
Released to return home
Leaving Young Lord Ellesmere
Despite how fond I've grown.

One day he'll see a likeness
In the mirror looking back,
And realise his father
Is a Scottish groom called Mac.

****

Geneva has a plan

I will not bloody do it!
He's older than you papa
Your selling me into marriage
I hate you – there you are!

You – you do not love me!
If you did, you wouldn't have this plan
The 8th Earl of Ellesmere
Is a disgusting lewd old man.

I know we're short of money,
I know we need some cash,
Why not sell some horses
Or put Isobel on the bash !

I had dreams of marriage
To a handsome wealthy beau.
The 8th Earl of Ellesmere
Is wealthy, but he's horrid
And he's old.

But if I must do this thing
To save the family fortunes
I will not give in gracefully
There's a man I will importune.

That groom they call Mackenzie
Now he looks a bit hot
He's big and strong and handsome
A dark horse – is he not.

I know he has a history,
I heard it from Lord John
He came with him from Ardsmuir
He has secrets .. Not for long!

Mackenzie's not his real name
My father said he lied
He was on the field at Prestonpans
The day my brother died.

But his eyes are kind
His voice is soft
When he talks to the horses
I think I'll get him into bed
Two weeks AFTER my courses.

****

The 9th Earl – Willie

BANG!!
Is the first sound I remember
And then silence seemed so long
I was not frightened by the sound
Then someone held me strong.

My parents died when I was born
My family was fractured
Grand pa, Grandma, my aunt, Lord John.
A new family – manufactured.

And always in the background,
When I was really small,
Was Mac the groom
So quiet, and calm, and strong, and really tall.

Mac taught me things, he told me NO
Without him being admonished
Firm and kind and always fair
But in fear of being punished.

I learned to ride – Mac taught me well
I learned respect for horses.
Til I was six was always there
But drawn by other forces.

When I was six he broke my heart
I saw him ride away.
He christened me James my papist name.
Before he left that day.

Years went by – and I grew up
But I never forgot.
And when we met on Frasers Ridge
It went through me like a shot.

This man my papa John calls friend.
Plays chess with and admires
I'm sure that he is Mac the groom
Why does he not recognise

He did not look back that awful morn
He caused me so much pain.
I asked him why?
He thought that we would never meet again.

A papist name, a rosary, a wooden snake
Were all he had to give
I won't tell him, but I treasure them
As long as I shall live.

****

Finding Jamie

Frank was dead, and history said
Jamie was alive.
Though he had gone back to die,
He managed to survive.

One officer of Frasers,
Survived that awful day
Was not executed,
Was spirited away.

We tracked him through the records
And the history books
An outlaw, then a prisoner
indentured to a Duke.

Then lost him in the wilderness
Of him there was no trace
To be so close, but far away.
Hope had been erased.

A snip of conversation,
A random line of Burns,
A pamphlet in a library file.
On these my future turned.

A printer now in Edinburgh
Still against the Crown.
But I could go back and find him
Roger had tracked him down.

With my affairs in order
No ties left behind
Brianna sent me with good grace
Her father, I should find.

And so I reached the print shop
He was standing at the press
Broad of shoulder, red of hair
I was scared I will confess.

I watched as he went ashen
And then began to weep
His legs gave way, quite gracefully
He collapsed into a heap.

We clung on to each other
Checking both were flesh
I wept tears of unchained joy
He cried with happiness.

We burned into each other,
How then would we start
To patch a hole two decades wide.
Two lives lived years apart.

He promised to be truthful
I had nothing there to hide.
He told me things in little bits,
Like driftwood on the tide.

In my mind I did the jigsaw
Of the pieces of his life.
I later found he'd missed a piece.
The one which was his wife!

How could I forgive him
This was treachery complete.
That woman tried to have me burned
A bitch skilled in deceit.

Confronted by his love for me
She shot him in the arm
It was me that she was aiming for.
But he would not have me harmed.

I listened to him talking
Could not apply a balm
To never ending grieving
And a mind he could not calm

How he tried to live a normal life
And married without thinking
To please his sister Jenny
He must have done it drinking.

And so we started over.
No longer in our youth
With a love that's shared when two souls bared.
Agree to tell the truth.

✳✳✳✳

Thoughts in Print

A day like any other day,
A respectable façade,
A cover for my murky trade
To make detection hard.

The web I weave around myself.
To hold it all together,
Is born of lies and of deceit.
It won't stand much more weather.

I tried to live the settled life
I tried to love another,
Her children are my family,
But I can't live with their mother.

So I open up the print shop
And settle to my work
Pen has more power now than sword.
Print more power than dirk

Thought nothing of the chiming door
Thought Geordie was returning
Chided him for taking time
My irritation burning.

A voice not heard for twenty years
But still a clear as bells
Spoke from above and put my thoughts
In seven kinds of hells.

That voice embodied in a face
And a form not an illusion.
Threw my fragile web of lies
Into a mass confusion.

For twenty years I have not slept
Without thought of her returning
For twenty years I kept alive.
Her memory, and the yearning.

And here she is, a real thing
Not seen through a fever
A living, breathing, solid Claire
Who I have loved forever.

I felt the blood drain from my face,
My legs went weak for sure
The ale pot fell before me,
And beat me to the floor.

How do I start to tell her
Of the mess that is my life
That in the time she was away
Laoghaire became my wife.

Claire is all for honesty
But I know that I must lie
God I need to hold her tight.
And pray she does not fly

I will tell her bit by bit
Of most that I have done
The tangle which is now my life
And pray she does not run.

****

Kidnapped

Young Ian swam to silkie isle
For the contents of the box
I saw him through the spyglass
Climbing up the rocks

Hid behind the island
Sails unfurled in the lee
A foreign ship ! what brought it here?
With a flag of Portuguese.

Ian thrown into the boat
Like a bag of bones.
That was what they'd come for
The gold and precious stones

We watched helpless from the headland
As she sailed off to the west
Destined for some foreign land
With Young Ian as a guest.

The clansman said that gold was cursed
Protected by the witch
Belonged to the Mackenzie
And she would return for it.

My blood ran cold, at my next step
To follow across the sea,
To rescue Ian and send him home,
From wherever he may be.

A ship from cousin Jared,
A cargo for Jamaica.
For that was where that ship was bound,
And we must overtake her.

I swallowed hard, my stomach turned.
Could I stay alive,
For three months on a pitching deck
Spewing o'er the side.

****

Acupuncture

I'd been throwing up for days,
I did not feel verra well,
I'd drunk a lot of ginger tea,
And still I felt like hell.

I cannot sleep for heaving,
If I eat I chuck it,
Ye cannot feel like living
With yer head inside a bucket

Willoughby is a strange one,
Keeps hit talents hid,
Says he has a Chinese cure,
If I do as he bids.

He produced a box of needles,
Thin and made of gold,
Where was he going to stick them,
That thought sent me cold.

I look like a porcupine,
I don't ken what that is,
Must be a rare strange animal,
With a face that looks like this!

But on the morrow, I am not green.
I'm not puking in the sea.
I'll break it to Claire gently
That I do not need her Tea.

****

156

The Porpoise

You don't argue with a seventy four,
She could blow us out the water,
Jamie's protests all for naught,
We hove to, like we oughter!

Bound also for Jamaica,
She wasn't pressing crew,
There was a form of plague on board.
A doctor was their due.

So I went aboard the Porpoise,
It's crew were full of fever,
Typhoid is a killer,
I knew I couldn't leave her.

A quiet lad, he does his job,
A helper I have found,
At 14 in the Navy,
God bless Elias Pound.

Intelligent and helpful,
With quiet and shrewd remark
Helps to keep the crew alive,
He really made his mark.

The fever cured, the ship now clean
The crew regained some pride,
Elias Pound lay down to sleep,
And in his sleep he died.

I sewed Elias in his shroud,
White from head to toes,
Tucked in his lucky rabbits foot
And put the last stitch through his nose.

****

Father Fogden

Brave or really stupid,
I'd jumped into the sea,
Floated with the current,
To a beach, and I was free.

Where was I ? I had not a clue?
This plan was really daft.
To get me to Jamaica,
First I must find a craft.

I wandered in the jungle,
Was bitten bad by ants,
No water and no sunscreen,
This holiday is pants !

I came round tied down to a bed!
My legs were sorely itching,
What is this place, it's really weird,
My get out button is twitching.

He's talking to a coconut!
He asks it for advice,
It says that I can't leave too soon,
Cos the weathers not too nice.

This man of some religion,
Has really lost his marbles,
Must be the hemp he's smoking,
Makes him really garbled.

But there is a wreck upon the shore,
A sailor killed his goat,
A little slant eyed Chinese man,
That's Willoughby, I thought.

And there they were, on the beach
Just packing up and leaving,
I might just catch the Artemis,
But distance is deceiving.

I wave and shout, he cannot hear
I will be left behind.
But he sees my signal flash,
Thank god my loves not blind !

Father Fogden held a wedding,
For a couple on the sand,
The form a bit impromptu,
The sentiment quite grand.

Father Fogden is a strange man.
Of that there is no doubt,
But he blessed us too,
In his own way,

His faith still quite devout.

****

Lord John gets it Right

Governor of Jamaica,
Seems a fair promotion,
Just five thousand miles away,
A mere hop across an ocean.

My welcoming reception,
I'm dressed up in full fig
When I spot Jamie Fraser,
And what is that ?...a wig!

Much as I admire the man,
He's always bringing trouble,
Ah – here come HMs marines,
At the bloody double.

He is again a wanted man,
But they've no written proof,
No warrant to arrest him,
I'm thinking on the hoof.

The ambitious little upstart,
With only acting rank,
Who comes to take him prisoner,
Is a nuisance if I'm frank.

I pull out my best disdain,
And put him to the test
Leftenant! When not on your ship
Where's your power to arrest.

Your power is only out at sea,
It ended on the dock,
Now kindly leave my friend alone,
You jumped up little cock !!

✳✳✳✳

Ian's Rescue

We landed in Jamaica
Storm swept, bruised and battered,
The Artemis dismasted,
Hers sails mostly in tatters.

With Jamie on the wanted list,
We must avoid the Navy,
And that temporary Captain.
Who is dishing out the gravy.

Is Ian on the Island,
Taken as a slave,
Our mission is to find him,
Before he meets his grave.

The Governors reception
Moves our mission on,
A get out of jail free card,
Written by Lord John.

What is Geilis Duncan
Doing on this Isle,
A good three husbands later
She's doing it in style.

The cave was called Abandawe,
It's a portal like the stones,
Ian was her sacrifice,
She'd turn him into bones.

She would not take my nephew,
I'd guard him with my life,
It was me that cut her head off.
With a sugar cutting knife

****

Drowning

A wave as high as all the masts
Swept me o'er the side,
Snagged on the metal from a spar,
I really should have died,

Floating down, endless peace,
I could not fight the feeling,
Embrace the everlasting light,
A wondrous sense of healing,

Just breathe in, and all is well
Fold the swell around you,
And god will put your earthly soul
Right back where he found you.

The feeling breaks, the rope is cut
I'm held in his embrace,
Breath is shared, his and mine,
Upwards now we race.

I had the choice to take that breath,
It would have been my last
Drowning is a peaceful way,
To make peace with your past.

Twas he who would not let me leave,
Twas he who gave me breath
His love for me will never see
Me meet a watery death.

****

Shipwrecked

Washed up on a distant shore
The ship around us broken
Strewn on sand , where is this land,
The land that god has chosen.

I don't know why I'm breathing,
I'm pretty sure I drowned,
A never ending weightlessness,
Then Jamie all around.

Are there more survivors,
Or are we the only two.
Have we lost all our family,
Is there only me and you.

Yes there were survivors,
And our bedraggled band,
Has reached the coast of Georgia,
God ,has had a hand.

Scotland seems so long ago
Oh so far away,
Time to see what lies in store
We've reached the USA.

****

Things you win at dice

I was in a bar in Wilmington
Tied up to a wall
My owner was playing dice
And losing – I recall

I had my head down on my paws
But I wasn't asleep
My ear was cocked and listening
In case I had to leap.

I'd never had an owner
Keep me more than a few days
I'm half a dog and half a wolf
With antisocial ways.

Oh here comes my new one
He's nothing but a lad
He seems to be quite proud of me
Things can't be all that bad

He's going to call me Rollo
Rollo of the dice.
I've never had a name before
I think that's really nice.

Oooh he has a family
This is what I need
They know I can catch my own fish
I'm really cheap to feed.

I am now a Fraser
The Frasers are my pack
Ian is my master
I'm never looking back.

Burying Hayes

Hayes was dead, I saw him hanged
At his last he saw a friend,
So full up wi whisky
He didna feel the end.

A superstitious bugger
He feared the dark at best
The churchyard was the proper place
To lay his bones to rest.

We gave him a fair send off
In the Gaelic sung some songs
With his body in the wagon
Left Charleston to the throng.

The Priest had wanted paying,
Of flesh he'd have his pound,
To rest a sinner like old Hayes
In consecrated ground.

'Twas dusk when we left Charleston
A shovel had been bought.
We picked a spot beside the wall.
That Hayes would like, we thought.

He was hiding in my wagon,
Still fettered up for hanging,
Scairt Young Ian witless,
When his chains they started clanging.

He talked the talk, he was a thief
a friend of Hayes, ye ken
Condemned to hang for smuggling.
And I was taken in.

By candle light we dug Hayes grave,
We didn't tell the priest,
Buried him and said a prayer.
At rest now at least,

Hayes now safely in the ground
We must resume our journey,
The wagon should be empty now
Not acting as a gurney.

He talked me into freeing him,
I would not hand him in,
Shook my hand and thanked me.
And parted with a grin.

I miss judged the Irish bastard,
With his easy line in charm.
I should have seen it in his eyes
He only meant us harm.

✳✳✳✳

Robbed

All aboard the Sally Anne,
We headed up the river,
Despite the lack of any waves,
Jamie's insides were aquiver.

All of our belongings
Were loaded on this boat,
Nothing else here to our name,
I hope we stay afloat.

The river seems so peaceful
Lush ground on either side,
All of mother nature
Undisturbed, as on we glide.

A beautiful and wild land,
Where anyone may roam,
Four travellers and a half wolf dog,
Where will we find a home.

At dusk ,we tied up for the night.
We thought it safe from harm,
Twas Rollos growl and barking
Sounded the alarm.

They stormed the cabin in a mob
Even Jamie could not fight
Knife to his throat, four pinned him down,
Struggle as he might.

They knew we had those gem stones,
They searched him to his skin
Found what they were looking for,
And then did not give in.

What they did not take they broke,
My surgeons kit and things
The leader of these vile men
Tried to steal my rings.

I took them off quite gracefully
And held them in his sight
Then rammed them hard into my mouth.
And swallowed them in fright.

I bit his hand as it searched my mouth
His fingers on my tongue,
He made me spit the rings back out
But I had swallowed one.

The one he stole meant all to me
But wasn't worth a lot.
Twas the Iron one, from Jamie
From the key to Lallybroch.

I recognised that Irish brogue
His voice an evil sonnet,
I would not forget that night
At the hands of Stephen Bonnet

We arrived at Aunt Jocastas,
With nothing to our name.
But the clothes that we stood up in,
And the will to start again

****

Aunt Jocasta

Don't be fooled by Aunt Jocasta,
She's Mackenzie through and through,
She'll walk you down her winding path.
And her will she'll have you do.

There's always an agenda,
Hiding in the wings,
A wee wee scorpion hiding there,
A most poisonous of stings.

But she is my kinfolk,
I have to play along,
Until the bit where I get hit,
Then things may go wrong.

When she lost her daughters,
They were on the run,
The gold under the carriage,
Is what built RiverRun.

She wants to leave an empire,
Legacy she craves
But I'll not be having anything,
Built on the back of slaves.

I cannot think ill of her,
She is lonely, needs a man,
She knows she cannae move my mind
I have my own plan.

The Mackenzie blood is deep in her,
She schemes just like her brother,
I cannot see it all as fault,
She looks just like my mother.

****

Bear Killer

Horses hobbled for the night,
A view fit to admire
We thought to cook the fish I'd caught
And lie down by the fire

It came out of the bushes,
Beady eyes a gleaming,
Lips pulled back to show its teeth,
Snot from its muzzle streaming.

I just had time to grab my Dirk
And push Claire out the way,
When dense black fur ran over me,
I thought it was my day,

Savage teeth , raking claws,
It's smell was fit to choke!
I wrestled for my life with it,
In its rage at being awoke.

Then smack! The world went silver
I let out a shout,
My ever helpful, loving wife,
Had hit me with a trout.

****

Finding the Ridge

We couldn't live with owning slaves,
We turned down River Run,
Aunt Jocasta would soon find
A man, to get her business done.

We'd take up on a land grant,
But that would come with strings
Tryon wanted military men,
Amongst other things.

We headed for the mountains,
To find a patch of land,
A place where we could put down roots,
A place to make a stand.

Sheltered in the woodland
Not far from a stream
Fish and game in plenty,
It was a settlers dream,

And emerging from the forest,
It's beauty made me shiver,
Trees as far as the eye could see,
flat land along the river.

My farmers eye loved everything,
It had a special feel,
And finding Fraser strawberries,
Seemed to seal the deal.

We'd need to sign the papers
And mark out all the ground.
A great big patch of paradise
Frasers Ridge was found.

****

Lizzie

Travelling to the colonies,
I didn't need a maid,
I was waiting on the dockside,
With my passage paid,

Her father owed some money,
Said another man would fetch her
He'd rather her across the world,
Than indentured to a letcher.

So there's me and Lizzie now,
Travelling cross the sea.
It's more me looking after her,
Than her looking after me.

Lizzie is a simple soul,
She's not seen much of life,
She's handy with the sewing,
But useless with a knife.

She likes to feel needed,
Tries hard to get things done,
But Lizzie Wemyss is terrified,
Life experience – she has none.

She's like a wounded puppy,
She follows me around,
Sometimes I'd like some kind of space
Where I just can't be found.

And then there's her bad habit,
Of jumping to conclusions,
She thinks the worst of everything,
This sometimes means confusion.

Like, she said Roger raped me
She told that to my Da!
Jamie beat him senseless,
The Indians took him far!

But Lizzie is forgiven now,
She had my best at heart.
She loves this mixed up family
Of which she is a part

****

On finding my father

The journey has been long and hard
Last night I went to hell
I was livid with my Roger
I told him to go as well.

I saw my mothers iron ring
On that Irish bastards hand
I knew that I must get it back.
It was Jamie's wedding band

He wouldn't take any payment
How was I so blind
He assaulted me and raped me.
He said payment was 'in kind'.

Next day when Lizzie woke me
I ran down to the dock
But Rogers boat had sailed away
Leaving me in shock.

Here comes Lizzie running now
Excited – in a flap.
I'm not in the mood for this
Lizzie – cut the crap

I've spoken to a man she says
A man who knows the score
A woman healed a man with surgery
At the play last night – theres more.

Her husband is called Fraser
He's down there by the store
Oh my god it's got to be
My parents I am sure.

I go down to the saloon
I'm directed round the back.
There's a big man with a pony tail
Standing down the track.

He's standing with his back to me
He's well over six feet tall
Broad shouldered and with bright red hair
Pissing up against the wall.

He senses me behind him
Looks back in surprise
It's like looking in the mirror
God I have his eyes.

His look is all suspicion
He thinks I am a whore.
He tells me he is married.
Well I knew that before.

He's finished what he's doing
And turns to walk away
'You are Jamie Fraser –
I hesitantly say.

My name is Brianna, I'm your daughter
Comes out next.
He pulls up sharp
His next breath whistles through his chest

His sharp blue eyes were filled with tears
He shook and then gave a sigh.
I guess it was the first time
I saw my father cry.

****

A Fish out of water

An Amazonian woman, With a mass of ginger hair,
A smile like potted sunshine, And a very blue eyed stare.
Stood upon my doorstep,
I fell in love right there.

An old fashioned history professor
Who sings and plays guitar,
I'm sure this six foot angel
Is out of my league by far.

If I could see my future,
would my life include,
A journey through the veil of time.
To a place where life was crude.

I cannot make a shelter
I'm a crap shot with a gun.
In the Carolina back woods
Life wouldn't be much fun.

But I would follow my Brianna
Through the mist of time.
To be half killed by her father
For a crime that wasn't mine.

Her father would involve me
In minor feuds and wars
A random swarm of locusts
And helping him hang doors

I got stuck at Alamance
The wrong side of the beck
Lucky me – I survived
When they hanged me by the neck.

I came good with Jamie
When he was bitten by a snake
I refused to let him die
He pulled through for goodness sake

I came to love the Frasers
To call the ridge my home
A big extended family
I never knew my own.

The fact that I can travel
Is really quite a bitch
Turns out I'm the offspring
Of the war chief and the witch.

We tried it just the one time
To come back through the stones
But they wouldn't send us anywhere
When we thought of home.

We ended where we started
The place we thought as home
A place of peace and drama
Of violence and calm.

The place to bring up children
Without a modern fridge
I expect Bree can invent one
Up on Frasers Ridge.

The adventure of a lifetime!!

How Ian Murray knew me
I really had forgot.
He had remembered everything.
I would rather not.

A teenage boy of privilege
Travelling with papa.
Taken to the back woods.
Sleeping under stars.

Used to getting my own way,
Spoiled and loud and brash.
If Mac the groom had been there
I'm sure my arse he'd thrash.

We called upon the Frasers.
Papa sought to find
The great tall red haired Scotsman.
Who lived inside his mind.

A cabin in the forest
Basic with no frills,
Papa seemed to love it
It just gave me the chills.

My first shock was – that Scotsman,
He was Mac the groom.
But he would not recognise me
When I stepped into the room.

How is he called Fraser now
How has he a new life
I did not believe him
When he said he had a wife.

And oh that evil smelling shed
I'd rather use a pot
I'd never been in such a thing
And I'd really rather not.

And I fell in that dank dark hole
The contents........ no mistake.
Covered me from head to foot
And then there was the snake

Even Papa teased me.
When they pulled my from that place.
And everyone recorded
The look upon my face.

Ian Murray saw it.
And remembered what he saw
The blazing eyes, the Fraser stare,
His Uncle to the core.

Filthy , stupid, angry
Venomous frustration
Falling in a privy is,
Complete humiliation

✳✳✳✳

Being Willie.

My brain feels like it's going to burst,
Seems everyone but me,
Knew just who my real father is
And my family history.

My mother, well I knew she died,
Just as I was born
They told me she was headstrong,
treated everyone with scorn.

My father, 8th Earl Ellesmere.
I bear his name for sure,
But twas he who called me bastard,
And called my mother whore.

Grandmama and Grandpapa
Did their level best,
To hide from me the awful truth
Well known to the rest.

Lord John and Isobel ,my aunt
Raised me from a child
Taught me how to be an Earl,
Stopped me from running wild.

Why do I remember that
The happiest times for me
Were the Stables at Helwater
Mac the groom and me,

He taught me how to love the land
He taught me how to ride
Taught me to swear in Gaelic!
I repeated it with pride!!

I was like his shadow
Until the awful day
Mac packed up his belongings
My hero rode away.

I cried for him for days and days
I wished him to come back,
I didn't think I'd see again
The groom they all called Mac.

I started hearing rumours
It wasn't very pleasant,
People started to remark
I don't look like my parents.

Mac was not his real name
He came to us from prison
Now he was in the colonies,
How were his fortunes risen.

I have his height, I have his build
I have his steel blue gaze.
His cheekbones and his sloping nose,
Looks I cannot erase.

The dawn of recognition,
Cut me like a razor,
When I shave and I look up
I'm shaving Colonel Fraser.

Did he rape my mother,
Or was she just a whore?
Sleeping with the servants
Or is there something more.

He claims responsibility
For the fact she died,
He won't speak any ill of her.
He'll not say more – I've tried.

Pride won't let me speak to him,
Nor the hurt that I remember
And the other thing I have from him
Is a red hot Fraser temper.

✳✳✳✳

The White Sow

She was the dearest piglet,
Wriggly and pink.
But always up to mischief,
She quickly learned to think.

We kept her longer than we should,
For we were quite mistaken,
That she would join our family.
That pig should have been bacon.

A streak of independence.
Every day she would escape,
Leaving a trail of destruction.
And carnage in her wake.

The list of things she's eaten
Is getting quite impressive
Jamie's hat, Briannas drawers,
That pig gets more aggressive.

Growing bigger every day,
Now with piglets of her own,
She got to choose just where she went.
Or her wrath would soon be known.

She does exactly as she likes,
She scares the pants off men,
No amount of food enticement
Will keep her in a pen.

Even the Indians respect her.
The white sow from the ridge,
I'm sure she'd have been bacon.
If we'd only had a fridge.

****

Regulators

Taxes are the curse of life
Yet they must be paid,
Used to run the Government,
And the money not waylaid.

Collected up by honest men
Who only take what's due
And not diverted to the pockets
Of the corrupt and powerful few.

But the rich who run the Country
Are greedy to the core
Will take the food from honest men
And then they ask for more.

Dishonest men all on the take
Collect the revenue,
They levy more than a man can make
And then they add their due.

A lot of us were sent here,
As punishment ye ken.
And now we have our freedom back
We won't be chained again.

Don't boast about your mansion
Fit to host the King and Queen
Built with our tax money.
Your morals are obscene.

We will band together
And fight for tax that's fair.
You may not see it coming
But a war is in the air.

****

Goats and Hell

Josiah told us where it was
The cabin in the wood
It stank of goat, it stank of hell
It stank of nothing good.

Dark and uninviting,
How could anyone survive,
In a rundown hovel in the trees.
Was anyone alive.

Ahoy the house, we called out,
Jamie held the gun.
No answer, was there no one there,
Had everybody run.

A face came to the window,
Threatening but afraid,
A woman, worn by hardship
From the righteous path had strayed.

To buy the twins their freedom,
The reason for this call.
What was in this house of horrors,
Really capped it all.

She had tortured old man Beardsley,
Just keeping him alive,
Enough to let him feel the pain.
Of burns he could survive.

He must have been a cruel man
Death would be a blessing,
I left that one to Jamie,
With my oath I'll not be messing.

Oh God, Mrs Beardsley,
My grin is not of mirth,
Her waters have just broken,
The woman's giving birth !!

She did not take her baby,
When she left at dead of night
She found the Twins indentures,
And was gone before the light.

Wrapped up with her half cast child,
The deeds to Beardsleys land,
Someone would find a home for her,
With inheritance, understand.

We buried old man Beardsley
Underneath a tree,
Alongside all his other wives,
I think I counted three.

We took the rest to Brownsville,
The baby and the goat
The hungry mite, foraging
Down the front of my old coat.

I often think of Fanny,
For that is what they called her,
When we left her there in Brownsville,
As their adopted daughter.

****

Bitten by a Snake

I didn't see it coming,
But an exploded powder keg
Of pain went through my body
As it flowed into my leg.

My eyes were on the buffalo
It was a big mistake.
To not look all about me -
I didn't see that snake.

It's poison slowed my senses
I felt myself go cold.
But my leg was throbbing hot as hell
Fever taking hold.

I couldn't walk, I couldn't crawl,
Could barely raise my head
If Roger couldn't get me home.
I'd verra soon be dead.

Roger Mac !now is the time
To really show your worth,
Me dying in the bushes
Is not a time for mirth.

He made me stay quite quiet
He prayed for me a bit.
In English not in Latin
The Presbyterian twit!

He built a sledge of branches
And dragged me from the wood
Until they came to look for us,
I didn't think he could.

Roger never gave an inch
Though I was racked with pain
He cursed me and cajoled me.
As the poison coursed my veins.

Claire was clearly frightened,
She wasn't making jokes.
Her cheerful bedside manner
A nervous, see through, hoax.

So she filled the hole with maggots,
And made me drink her broth.
She thought I couldn't see the saw
She hid under the cloth.

I'd rather die a whole man
Than live with half a leg
She'll not touch me with that saw.
No matter how she begs.

She could not inject me,
For lack of a syringe.
My arse was safe from needles,
Though the maggots made me cringe.

Stubborn and rebellious
I'd die a proper man
With two whole legs, and all my bits.
At least that was the plan.

And I'd die in my own bed
With my wife beside me.
I'm going out a happy man,
With God alone to guide me.

A determined woman is my wife
I turned back from the light
When she said she needed me
That's when I chose life.

And my daughters swift invention
Came neatly to the pass
I'd rather Claire jabbed a needle
Than that snakes fang in my arse.

✳✳✳✳

Rape

No good comes from Brownsville
And all of it's called Brown,
They all know how to bear a grudge
And Lionel wears the Crown.

A violent and a cruel man
He loves a good vendetta
He doesn't like the Frasers,
I think he should know better.

Taken from the surgery
A bag upon my head,
Trussed up like a turkey
Sure I'd soon be dead,

The still was a diversion
To draw the men away.
Lionel Brown had sworn he would
Be back another day.

The vile names they called me,
They are skilled at abuse,
To violate a woman
They don't need an excuse.

The Brown gang took their turns at me.
Then tied me hand and foot
They left me there so I would die.
An ant under his foot,

I lost myself in music,
Escaped into my head,
Tried to find a happy place
While all my reason fled.

My rescue wasn't pretty,
Military in its precision.
No reprieve, kill them all.
I heard that last decision.

One survived the rescue,
That was Lionel Brown.
They took him to the Surgery
And there they tied him down.

I was lost inside my shell,
My outside wounds would heal,
The bruises very soon would fade
The open wounds would seal.

Once, Jamie said his Inner man
Laid bare, had hurt his soul
And Had to build a shelter
Before it could be whole.

With Lionel in my surgery
With Marsali by his bed,
Mentally I found some wood.
And started on my shed.

****

I've Taken no Such Oath

My mother called her English whore,
My mother called her bitch,
Had her tried at Cranesmuir.
Wanted her burned, a witch.

I remember well the big stramash,
When Claire came back for daddy,
My mother tried to shoot him
She was In such a paddy.

I've lived with them for many years,
I see they love each other,
And now I've come to look at Claire
As if she were my mother.

When they came and kidnapped her,
They knocked me to the floor,
I am heavy still with child,
Yet still they called me whore.

Claire has taught me many things
Of the art of healing,
The thought of healing Lionel Brown
Is not that appealing.

I prepared for him a potion,
I told him it would heal.
If he lay still and drank it,
Then he'd have a meal.

He would not have to drink it,
I did not have to check,
With one swift move I jabbed it,
Into the big vein in his neck.

His death was almost instant
Quicker than a gun,
Claire's oath said she'd not harm him
But I've not taken one !

****

The Coming Storm

It's nice to have a normal day,
One without a drama,
Boring domestic humdrum
Seems to make me calmer.

There's heavy weather coming
I hear the distant thunder,
Lightening forking from the sky,
A divine signal, I wonder.

I know unrest is coming
There will be a war,
I know that he will fight it,
Of that I know I'm sure.

I will pack up and go with him,
Be an army wife.
I could not bear to lose him now,
This man who is my life.

****

Taking Stock

Ten toes, two feet
Two legs - that's neat
Nearly lost one of those.

Fingers – nine
But that's just fine,
If the rest work – I suppose.

Two arms to hold the one I love,
One heart – still beating- strong

One chest – where someone's head can rest.
To check the heart has not gone wrong.

Two eyes – to see the whole of you
Not quite so sharp this year.

Two ears – they hear you laughing
A sound I love to hear

One nose to hold the scent of you
Two lips to tell you that........

The best bits are all working fine ....
Happy Birthday Sassenach!

✳✳✳✳

Bedtime Stories

Come sit here by your grand da's knee
Sit quiet and verra still
And I will tell you of my life
Listen if you will

I will tell you stories from
A long long time ago
And a lifetime of adventures
Ye ken I'll tell them slow

Put the plaid across my knees
Keep yer grand da warm.
Put more on the fire
Pour grand da a dram.

It all began back in a time
Before my hair was white
With the Bonnie Prince in 45
With the Jacobites.

I'll tell of Uncle Dougal
The War Chief of the Clan
Of my godfather old Murtagh
Exasperating man.

Of warriors like Angus... and Rupert
All long dead.
And a funny little lawyer
I believe he was called Ned.

I'll tell of English Redcoats
And American Revolution
Of History and Mystery
Of fighting and confusion.

And then there is abiding love
From family travelled far.
Tales of life on Frasers Ridge
And how I loved your dear Grandma

Sit by me now my little ones
And I will tell you slow
A story Once Upon a Time
200 years ago.

****

The End of My World

He is dead!
The world stopped turning!
I wasn't in control,
Surely, I would feel him missing,
Somewhere in my soul.

Drowned!
There is no coming back,
If he is lost at sea,
Surely there is some mistake,
I still feel him with me!

Lost!
I sit and watch the door,
But he will not come home,
This time, is he really gone,
Am I on my own

Grief!
Is such a little word,
For a feeling oh so large,
It occupies the whole of you,
With misery in charge.

Choices!
I think through all the methods
And the poisons, in my head.
What's the most effective way,
To render myself dead.

Comfort!
Pour the brandy,
I shall drink until I'm numb,
Deaden all my senses,
Surely sleep will come.

Company!
But I am not the only soul,
Who mourns his death alone,
Bring another bottle John.
Don't drink on your own!!

****

Forget me Not

When my body is no more
My bones are in the earth
Part of me will live with you,
Forever at your hearth.

I'm with you when you first awake,
Before your eyes adjust
A shadow in the half light,
You'll find me if you must.

When you go about your day to day
When your soul is bare
When you feel life is all too much
Then I will be there,

You'll breath in and you'll smell me
If you can't quite see
The shadow in the corner
Don't be scairt, it's only me.

When the evening comes around,
You sit upon the porch
And tell me all about your day,
I'm listening of course.

Listening attentively
As you tell your story
But I was still there with you,
Even though I've gone to glory.

And I will lie beside you
As you lay your head
Your pillow won't be lonely
With me inside your head,

Blue flowers on the hillside
In your dreams a Scot.
Make sure you don't forget me.
I will forget you not.

✳✳✳✳

Thank you
For your Support &
Riding For the Disabled
Best Regards
Maggie J

213

Made in the USA
Columbia, SC
08 May 2022

60015850R00129